AFRICAN BESTIARY

TALES OF SURVIVAL

POEMS & PAINTINGS | ALL AGES

WILLIS BARNSTONE

BLACK
WIDOW
PRESS

BOSTON

Black Widow Press is an imprint of Commonwealth Books, Inc. Distributed to the trade by Simon & Schuster throughout North America, Canada, and the U.K. Black Widow Press and its logo are registered trademarks of Commonwealth Books, Inc.

Joseph S. Phillips and Susan J. Wood, Ph.D., Publishers
www.blackwidowpress.com

Interior text production & design: Geoff Munsterman

Author photograph: Antoine Cuvelier

ISBN: 979-8-991-13914-4

Acknowledgements:

"The Whale" from *Bishop Theobaldus's Bestiary*, Translated from Latin by Willis Barnstone for Spiro Press, NY, 1964, jointly with Indiana University Press, Bloomington, IN, 1964. A boxed edition. "The Whale" in *Bishop Theobaldus's Bestiary*, New Directions, New York, 1999.

All paintings are original. I owe inspiration to Albrecht Dürer (1471-1528) for his engraving of the hippopotamus and to ancient Egyptian sculpture for the baboon and other paintings.

Ernest Hemingway goes on safaris until the last years of his life. He feels Africa's magic yet slays lions and wildebeests. His African hunting books lie on every field station book table. His last work is the memoir, *A Moveable Feast*. Let me say that for me to have lived in Africa for long periods and to paint and describe her beautiful beasts has been "A Moveable Feast."

to sons Robert and Tony Barnstone with whom I share long periods in Africa and daughter Aliki Barnstone there in spirit, and my wife Sarah Handler with me everywhere

TABLE OF CONTENTS

 GIRAFFE

 LION

 ELEPHANT

 CHEETAH

 GAZELLE

 ZEBRA

 LEOPARD

 FEVER TREE

 THORN TREE

 HIPPO-
POTAMUS

 RHINOCEROS

 RED
ELEPHANT

 BUFFALO

 CROCODILE

FLAMINGO

IBIS

GENET CAT

PAINTED DOG

MOSQUITO

GOOD
HUMAN
BEASTS
AROUND
EDEN TREE

CHIMPANZEES
SCREAM
IN TREES

BABOON,
EXPERT IN
FRIVOLITY

VERVET
MONKEY

COLOBUS
MONKEY

EDGAR
ALLEN
POE

OWL

ALEXANDER
THE GREAT'S
OWL

EGYPTIAN
OWL

 CAT  CATS

 HYENA  SNAKE

 SALVATION SAMMY  WARTHOG

 KILIMANJARO  FISH EAGLE

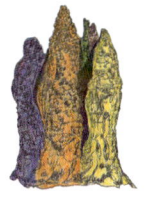 TERMITES  BOY SLAVE

 SPIDER  MAYAN STATUE

 GEOFFREY CHAUCER  DANTE ALIGHIERI

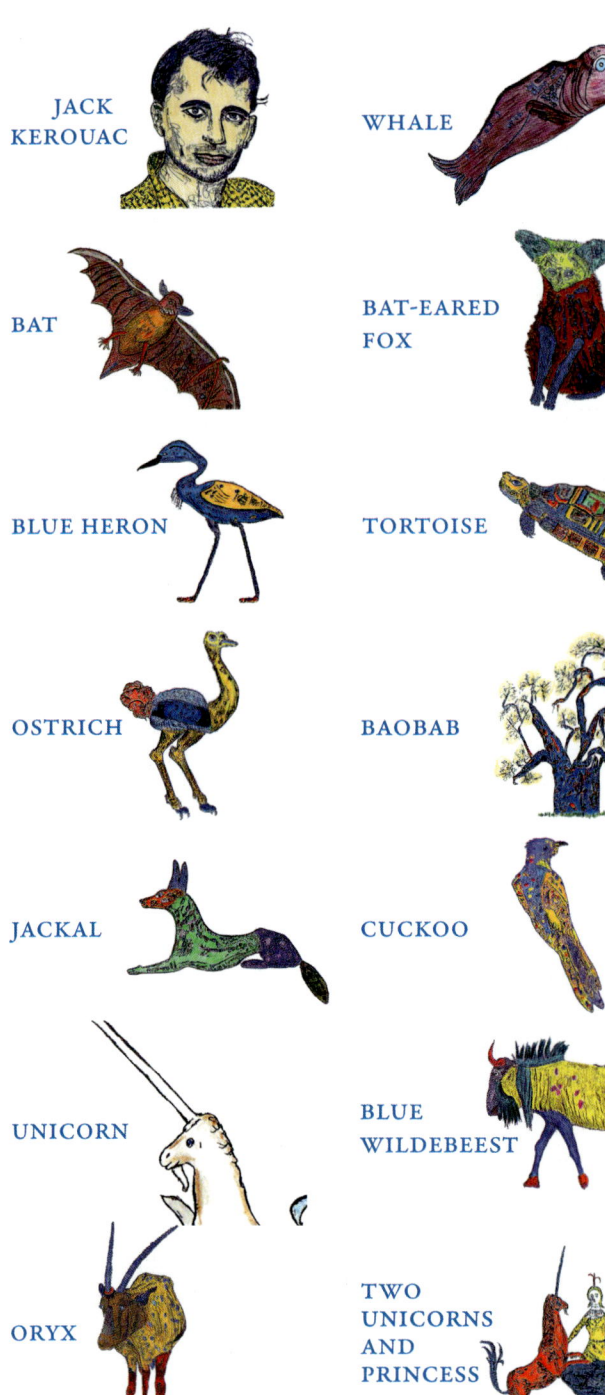

JACK
KEROUAC

WHALE

BAT

BAT-EARED
FOX

BLUE HERON

TORTOISE

OSTRICH

BAOBAB

JACKAL

CUCKOO

UNICORN

BLUE
WILDEBEEST

ORYX

TWO
UNICORNS
AND
PRINCESS

 GUINEA FOWL

 KINGFISHER BIRD

 DIKDIK

 LION

 FLY

 WILLIAM BLAKE

 VLADIMIR NABOKOV

 ANTOINE DE SAINT-EXUPÉRY

 RED BUTTERFLY

 BLUE BUTTERLFY

 GENIAL TIGER

 PEACOCK

 PARROT

 INDIAN TIGER

CHRISTOPHER SMART

PELICAN

HOODED VULTURE

CAMEL

ORANGUTANG

CHIMPANZEE

GORILLA

DWARF MONGOOSE

IMPALA

KUDO

WATERBUCK

GEMBOK

SWAN

PABLO PICASSO

 CHARLES
BAUDELAIRE

 AFRICAN
HONEYBEE

 DOVE

 COW

 WILLIAM
SHAKESPEARE

 ST. JOHN
OF THE
CROSS

 JUAN ANTONIO
DE LA PEÑA

 MIGUEL
DE CERVANTES

 GOLDEN
PANTHER

 LILAC-BREASTED
ROLLER

 GREEN HORSE

 BLACK
PANTHER

 DONKEY

 YELLOW
BUTTERFLY

YELLOW
HORNBILL

WATTLED
CRANE

SERVAL

ARDWOLF

NOCTURNAL
CIVET

KLIPSPRINGER

SABLE
ANTELOPE

BLUE
ANTELOPE

BONGO

AUSTERE PURPLE
GRENADIER

AFRICAN
CROWNED
CRANE

MARABOU STORK

KORI
BUSTARD

SCIMITAR
KNIFE ORYX

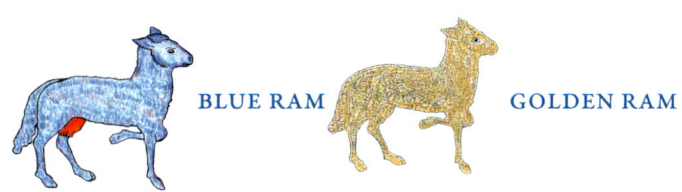

BLUE RAM   GOLDEN RAM

INTRODUCTION TO PARADISE

& TO PARADISE LOST

PARADISE

ANIMALS IN THE ANCIENT WORLD
& A MODERN CATASTROPHE

The most popular book in the world for two millennia before our century has been the Bible, a compendium teaming with animals. After Greco-Roman antiquity, the second most copied and read book in European languages was the Christian bestiary. From earliest times animal wisdom books were also popular in Egypt, Persia, India, Ethiopia, and China. Beast books were read aloud in every continent, books containing poems and illustrations.

Linked to the medieval bestiary were wondrous companion books: the lapidary, an illuminated book of precious stones; the aviary, an illuminated book of birds; the angelary, an illuminated book of angels. Each figure—be it sapphire, eagle, or the fallen angel Lucifer—comes with a picture, a descriptive tale, and an ethical explanation.

In the Hebrew Bible, one of Adam's first deeds is to give names to all the animals. In doing so, Adam participates in their Earthly creation. The original fateful names have been analyzed for the multiple meanings. The act of naming them also unites Adam to the beasts who, after the expulsion from the Garden, will forever be both domestic friends and wild enemies. The serpent is seen by later religions as an evil creation in Eden, causing human downfall. Or is the serpent, the snake, the source of human liberation?

Who is that serpent in the Hebrew Bible? He is Satan, God's attorney in snake attire. His unforgivable crime is giving Eve human qualities: knowledge, the power to disagree; to achieve exile, hardship, motherhood. And freedom. In her disobedience to restrictive codes, Eve is also the hero of us all. And Satan the snake is key to her achievements.

Humans descend from Eve and Adam. The serpent frees us from an eternal now to enter moving time, into reason, and eventually begin the feat of reading, writing and even inventing a Bible, Torah, whose first book, Genesis, begins with the words, יהי רוא (yehi or). Let light be! The serpent and Eve give us "the light of mind."

In other cultures, the snake is a very fine creature. In the Sumerian Ningizidda, the God of Life, and the Egyptian Uraeus serpent is used on the Pharaoh's forehead and also as a cobra on his headdress.

For the Greeks, the serpent represents "good health." He is depicted as a snake caduceus twisted around a pole. The caduceus is a symbol of healing in the Asklepian staff of the Greek god Asklepios, son of Apollo and founder of modern medicine.

For the Romans two snakes entwined around the caduceus, a short herald's staff, is a herald of the Hippocratic Oath that all doctors take.

Moses himself in Numbers 21:4-9 asks God for help in terrible times. The lord orders him to create a bronze statue of a snake so that those bitten by a plague of poisonous snakes might gaze on the statue and live. By reversing the essential nature of the snake from sinful to Creature with godly powers, he also momentarily suspends the prohibition of idolatry. He also permits his chosen people to adore a bronze statue and be saved by the serpent god. So, bestiary animals have an endless history and their duties in the world of humans change and change and change.

BIBLE ANIMALS, REAL & IMAGINARY

Both the Old and New Testaments are repositories of beast tales, the earliest form of which is the Jewish bestiary: Adam and his holy animal companions. In the Song of Songs, the dove floats over hills amid the lovers. We see Daniel tamer of lions, Jonah in the belly of the whale, the phoenix in Job. John of Patmos, author of The Book of Revelation (Apocalypse), uses animals, from lamb and bear to eagle and dragon in ordinary and in monster forms. They tell his tale of salvation. There were innumerable books published before and after printing emerged, using drawings and paintings of choice animals. Each beast is charged with metaphorical significance in episodes of cosmic warfare occurring in ancient Babylon. The tale of the battle with beasts is placed far in the past to conceal their own contemporary life-and-death struggles with the Roman Empire.

In Apocalypse the beasts—from lamb to dragon and the pale green horse of death—lead the good to joy the city of heaven with walls of jasper in a city whose walls are made of diamonds. But the wicked are cast forever into the doom of sulfuric fires. The sea monster Leviathan (Ezekiel 29:3) becomes in the deeply political Book of Revelation an extraordinary behemoth representing the terrible forces of Rome and its dragon-empowered emperors:

Then I saw a beast coming up from the sea,
With ten horns and seven heads and on his horns
Ten diadems, and on his head were the names
Of blasphemy. The beast I saw was like a leopard,
His feet like a bear and his mouth like the mouth
Of a lion. And the dragon gave him his power
And his throne and fierce power of dominion.

Rev. 14: 1-6

FABLES AND BESTIARIES

Forms of bestiaries pop up relentlessly in all periods. The scientific bestiary goes back in Europe to Aristotle's *Historia Animalium*, an extended treatise on 147 animals describing anatomy, development, and behavior. Many were the imitators, including Herodotos and Pliny the Elder.

The earliest traditional Western animal book was legendarily composed by Aesop (620?-560? B.C.), a slave on the Greek island of Samos. These didactic fables are later imitated by Jean de la Fontaine and Marianne Moore. But fables are of humans in animal dress, who by their animal behavior reveal a lesson in human behavior.

By contrast with fables, the bestiary is about real beasts in books of animal anatomy and habits to which is added a cautionary tale. Its composer is a naturalist, that is, one interested in the science of nature. The earliest naturalist is traditionally said to be an Alexandrian monk from the second or third century. His Greek title, Physiologos, means a naturalist or zoologist. Physiologos (Physiologus in Latin) eventually signified both the naturalist and the book he composed. As with Aesop of the fables, the original texts disappear.

The great period of the Christian bestiary occurs early as the 5TH century the Byzantine Middle Ages. It flourishes through most of Europe, the Levant and North Africa, and famously in Ethiopia, one of the earliest nations to claim Christianity. Vellum bestiaries are usually sewn together with lavish illustrations, including engravings, woodblocks, and illuminated color plates.  They describe animals in exotic detail, followed by a passage interpreting the tale's allegorical significance. Therein one is intended to hear the mystical meaning of God's word. The dove is a faithful woman, the ant a loyal worker member of the congregation, the lion is Christ who sleeps with one eye open to guard us lest we fall. The panther, who is the handsomest of quadrupeds, is another incarnation of the Christ:

Now Christ is the panther of our mystery,
And he exceeds all other men in beauty.
Gathering all he wished, he gratifies
His hunger. Then sleeps and saves us when he dies.

In the medieval world there is a prevailing notion of exact correspondences between the creator God and everything in his creation, from stars and planets and angels to humans, beasts, and even stones. We see some of these unbreakable circles of creation in the angelary, bestiary, and lapidary. So, each living beast—from fly and frog to lion and eagle—carries its own coded meaning. For example, in the Anglo-Saxon bestiary, the pelican tears open its breast to bring its young to life with its own blood. The pelican is a living animal representation of Jesus (Yeshua).

In these precious books the whale is the devil in the guise of a friendly accommodating sea creature. When sensual sailors on a foundering ship camp for safety on a whale's back, thinking it an island on the ocean where they can roast their meats, the whale quickly dives to the bottom and drowns the hapless sailors. The didactic punch: Anyone seduced by candied aromas from the devil-whale's monstrous mouth will sink and die:

> He who confides his hope in him is coarsely heaved
> Down into Hell and bitterly deceived.

OTHER BESTIARIES

Dante embeds metaphorical beasts in his *Commedia.* In the first cantos of *Inferno* we see a bear, a lion, and an eagle in the dark fearful wood. Leonardo da Vinci inserts his *bestiario* in his notebooks. And the animal genre remains popular in modern times, seeding the works of Lewis Carroll, T. H. White, and Jorge Luis Borges who gives us a mythical bestiary in his insuperable *The Book of Imaginary Beings.*

Guillaume Apollinaire wrote a splendid *Bestiare* that was illustrated by Raoul Duffy. Pablo Neruda composes a *Bestiario* for which Antonio Frasconi does color woodblocks. In these newer versions, God and the devil usually disappear, but the multivalent animals remain as historical and equally fantastic as in earlier holy incarnations. They serve the same pedagogical purpose of judging the *comédie humaine* through our animal counterparts.

One of the major surprises is the comic book artist who has returned to be the bestiary patron of animals. I say "returned" because many of the cartoonish drawings in the earliest bestiaries of linear woodblocks and engravings seem to leap over centuries of perspective paintings to find kinship with the new cartoon drawings, comic strips, and films. Walt Disney, Saul Steinberg, and other comic book artists, including Art Spiegelman, have made the animals narrate their period and their social and political message. Spiegelman is a master in universalizing his *maus* (mouse) in his holocaust survival tale. Through his mouse he immediately evokes Franz Kafka's Josephine who sings mesmerizingly to other mice in the walls where they hide from the hunter.

BISHOP THEOBALD'S BESTIARY

My first active experience with the traditional parabolic bestiary came in 1964 when I publish an English/Latin version of an eleventh-or-twelfth century illustrated Latin book, *The Bestiary of Bishop Theobaldus and the Natures of Twelve Animals* (Physiologus Theobaldi Episcopi de naturis duodecim animalium). The illuminated book was found in the Abbey at Monte Cassino and attributed to an Italian monk named Theobaldus. My translation appears as a boxed edition by the New York art book publisher Spiro Press and Indiana University Press, with color woodblocks and lithos by Ruddy Pozzatti. It later appeared without illustrations in my book *To Touch the Sky* (New Directions, 1999).

Theobald's *Latin Bestiary* (his Physiologus) is translated into Middle English and into the main European tongues in the twelfth to thirteenth century. The British Library's Arundel copy has rhyming couplets in which each line has an internal Leonine rhyme preceding the caesura. All this melodic trickery gives us wise and witty, scintillating naïve verse. In the poem on the whale, Latin *Cethegrande* for "whale" in Latin is imported into English:

> Cethegrande is a fis,
> The moste that in water is.

When Italian Theobald recreates the Homeric myth of the Siren as a Christian icon of wickedness and female deceit, his Siren no longer has a fish body but grotesque legs, and, as the Sirens in the *Odyssey*, is a among those who hear and will perish:

> Sirens are singing monsters of the sea,
> With many voices and varied melody.
> Often the reckless sailors passing near
> Are sung to sleep with sweetness in their ear;
> And ships are wrecked and all aboard are drowned.
> Although the mariners who perished found
> A lovely virgin from above the waist—
> Below, bird legs were monstrously misplaced.

AFRICAN BESTIARY

I keep the memory of the traditional bestiary when I walk the animal dominions of Africa, in southern Morocco, Nubian Egypt, Kenya, Lamu, Tanzania, and Zanzibar. This present bestiary has a moral import—social and ecological for the most part—though the pure beauty of the birds, quadrupeds, and creepers takes over and becomes its own primal message. The mosquito for me is the embodiment of evil, though I know this bug did not graduate from a nefarious academy of diabolism. With a push from Darwin, his survival genes, rather than criminal intent, have made it a killer. In the jungle, seeing the misery of old and young from malaria, I lost it and fulminated in "The Mosquito":

> The mosquito is a booming, lethal fly.
>   Our enemy,
> Leaving us limp. We shiver, burn, and die.
>   His industry,
>
> Malaria, is his weapon of dominion.
>   With a sting

He infects blood. Wicked force. By world opinion:
     He's a bloody being.

He is to be despised, swot and poisoned.
     The scientist
Explores all recent lanes of medicine
     Against the horrorist,

Whose mirco-bombs explode.
     He tolls the pain
Of continents. The old and young lie stowed
     Below the rain-

Forest mangroves where this criminal
     Leaves his parasite
In flesh. Only a vaccine might
     Deceive the virus. But none.

Swamp fly, we are lost. Join the jackals
     Entombed with the night Pharaoh.
Child killer, freeze to death on snow-blue
     Giant, Kilimanjaro.

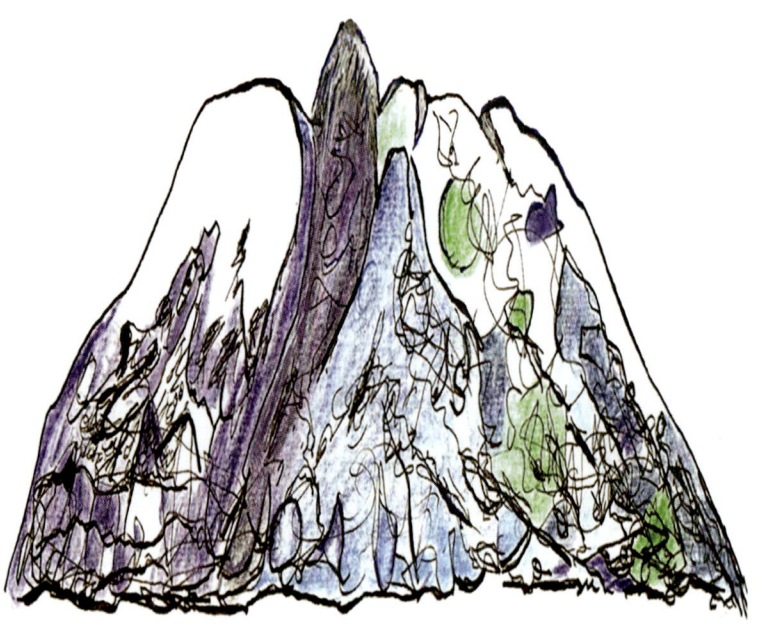

More cheerful and benevolent is the tiny dikdik, who is a perfect emblem of the wars of nature between the carnivore and herbivore. There is no need to moralize for either side of the hunger agon, but merely observe in the "Dikdik":

The dikdik is the smallest antelope
        No bigger that a fat tomcat,
Precious as the creation of small hope.
        When teeth are eager to make splat
Of you, alarmed, you swerve, dive and leap
        From jaws of carnivores
So, you won't be a quick quick tidbit heap
        Of tiny bones for a wild boar
Or cheetah in need of antipasto. You
        Are grace on paws, a ballet child
Among the pros, and as the Child you Too
        Are Father of us in the wild.

GUNS IN PARADISE

ECOLOGICAL WAR IN AFRICA

African Bestiary, which I began in continental Kenya, the sumptuous island of Lamu, and the alleys of Stone City in Zanzibar, has a relentless moral design. As noted, it contains information on the combat between carnivores and herbivores. More, it traces the ecological war between armed poachers and animal-protector rangers. The insanely increasing slaughter now casts doubt on the survival of all animals in bush and jungle. The battle to survive is the horror tale of Africa. Climate may be friend and adversary. Skies green or parch. But the homo sapiens, a sometime friend, is now the fatal enemy. The great protected parks are positive, with the caveat that poachers still invade, overwhelm, and kill, even from the air, bombing and machine-gunning the great animals. Cities expand their presence in the countryside, and so forests fall, savannas grow villages and metropolises, and thousands of species and millions of animals disappear.

The intruders also eat antelope, gorilla, and even crocodile. So the food poacher hunter also has a local market for his or her kill. The immediate danger comes from foreign powers, mainly Chinese, but the Vietnamese and Japanese are also into it. Hong Kong remains the biggest importer and distributor of ivory and refuses to join an international ban on marketing ivory. They have agreed in the past, but ignored the agreement. They arm poachers to provide customers with rare birds and quadrupeds, and with ivory tusks from elephants and rhinos for piano keys and sexual stimulants. Should these sub rosa ways of capture, smuggling, and murder continue, African animals of Earth, sky, and water may survive only in books and zoos.

Zoo derives from Greek for "life." Better for the animal dominion to roam life dangerously in the wild than to linger well-nourished in enlightened jails of foreign zoos. Africa is the world's

zoological heart. Humans and animals began there. Clearly, the bestiary heartland must survive and thrive in all its fullness. See the recent Academy Award nomination "Virunga: Gorillas in Peril," for a documentary on the forces that are slaughtering the extant gorillas. Statistics on devastation and spoliation of terrain are ghastly. In the last decades years the poachers have wiped out about ninety-five percent of the big animals. Conservationists writing in the *New York Times* suggest we have a few years before total extinction.

Compared to this havoc, Hemingway's nasty hunting expeditions are children playing games with toy pistols. I hope the pitiful plight of the marvelous beasts reaches good ears. If not, the continent where animal and human life began on our green and blue globe will be wasteland. As humans develop over the centuries, their civilizations have not been good news for animal nations. Those who are universally concerned with animal rights seldom cast their eye beyond urban environments. Original species in Africa are leaving us. Brave naturalists, conservationists, and the rangers, all with minimum resources do their best to slow apocalypse. Soon, we shall have little more than a memory of what was the populated Paradise of Eden.

Patricia Awori, a leader of The African Coalition. consisting of 24 African states, informs us:

> In 1979 there were an estimated 1.3 million African elephants. Today, only 470,000 remain; some authorities estimate the number to be considerably lower. The loss of a million elephants has been due primarily to killing for ivory. Natural habitat loss is a second important factor: human population has tripled in elephant range states since 1970.
>
> Major public awareness campaigns have been launched worldwide to save the elephant and halt the illegal trade in ivory.

For now, let us glance at and hear the living beasts on African lands, in equatorial air, at the hippo sleeping in shallow waters, who bolts across the night plains and through the forests like a wild RR train. Watch the philosophical giraffe, armed with giant legs, roam, his eyes always on threatening felines. Beware. The crocodile snaps at a fish or small boat, or loafs on a river rock, absorbing food from the sun, while inside its wide-opened mouth a small white bird cleans the debris from its teeth. And rest your eyes on the lion sleeping with one eye open. Soon she or he will leap and herbivore will become supper. This is nature's Darwinian battle of beast and beast. Unnatural is when the helicopter roars overhead and all members of the hippo clan and elephant herd and their trailing children are ripped to death in a storm of bullets. The contemporary habit of destroying African animal life must cease.

This work tells the wonder of each animal and asks for protection. It may help to understand and love each of these marveled beasts, from lone giraffe to gray crowned crane; from bat-eared fox to oryx on the scrub.

AFRICAN BESTIARY

TALES OF
SURVIVAL

POEMS & PAINTINGS

WILLIS BARNSTONE

GIRAFFE, GRAND PHILOSOPHER OF AFRICA

Twiga
Giraffa reticulate

The giraffe stands in huge gentility
      A solitary tower
On the savanna. Next to his family,
Brooding with silent power,
He guards the oaken-color plain against
The springing carnivore
Who wants his sleeping young for lunch. A fence
Of stone, this herbivore

Will not retreat. His eyes turn cruel. No sack
Of Disney gush, he glares
With globes of hate if predators attack.
      With blacksmith hoofs, he tears
Their feline eyes out, cracks their ribs. Don't mess
With the tall male giraffe.
For lion or lusty leopard who gives chase,
He wields his legs as staffs
To smash the enemy. When safe, he goes
      To a far hill where his troop
Of leaning towers treads the evening blue
Savanna. Now in the loop

Of war and peace, this giant stands in peace.
Keen in the twilight breeze,
A silent sly Diogenes from Greece,
Brooding in floating ease,
Our giraffe is the grand philosopher

Of Africa, good Plato
      Inscribed with spots of light near snouts of fear.
No underground potato,
The giraffe looms outdoors—never in caves—
      Where he's both sentinel
And sky dweller. His cloud-high eyeballs save
      His young from feline Hell.

The spy giraffe notes everything that is.
      Believe in her. She's wise
Like the grand elephant. Their threatened bliss
      Survives in mammoth thighs.
Now, a giraffe leans low, sprints from the herds three stars of grass.
On far hills see grace of the huge ground-bird
      Of floating steel and glass.

LION SLEEPS WITH ONE EYE OPEN

Simba
Panthera leo[1]

The lion sleeps with one eye open after dawn.
At night he prowls the plain and bush for pre
His third eye dreams he's Pharaoh on the law
Of the savanna where he wrestles in play.

In ancient days he poses in a cave
For wall painters who never make him shave
On Earth the monarch lion wakes by Sun
And with a mortal bite chokes a zebra for fun

And pride in gold ladies and cubs. One day
When Sun strolls on a cloud, with roar and play,
He leaps into the sky and with a mammoth bite
Gulps the Sunstar, blackening Earth to night.

The lion is the handsomest quadruped,
But watch out for this feline charmer in his pride
Who with a scream will turn a world to dread!
Tame killers, if you can, or keep them on your side.

1 Animal names are given in Swahili, the primary tongue of East Africa, and
   in their scientific Latin form.

ELEPHANT WITH SHOES OF SATIN

The elephant like whales is hugely smart
And phones her feelings over herbal plains.
She fears no living creature, yet a heart-
less gun will still her memory. The rains
Shampoo her mountain back. Before a stream
She tests the floor in ballet-pads as feet

And then in silence crosses in a dream
Through oceanic waterfall pools to defeat
Her roaming thirst. She swims for hours. Her brain
Is three times bigger than any man's.
Aspiring to dance on stars, the holy elephant
Smells Heavens. Listen to her cosmic chant.

If lions snare her calf, she fights and screams insane
While charging males joust tusk-to-tusk or use
Their proboscis like an airplane to snare
300 pounds of food from trees. Her twin-ears fan
The south wind into blowing North. Do not abuse
This monument of muddy beauty. Care.

Beware of Chinese Hemingways or the rich fool
Who claims ground ivory cures his languid tool.
The elephant is wisely kind to friends. Shakespeare
Composed her as blue goddess of our sphere.
At night she dances on stars. The holy elephant
Smells heavens. Listen to her cosmic chant.

GAZELLES ARE ROAMING STARS BENDING A WIND

Swala Tomi
Gazella thomsonii

The gazelle is the poet among beasts
On which each predator of grazers feasts.
She dances in the Song of Songs on hills,
Eating lilies. These mystic lovers thrill
And sleep in steep oblivion. Gazelles
Dance on the wind till Sun falls into wells.
But on the plains, the cheetah breaks her neck
And with his savage jaws soon she's a speck
Of what she was. Hyenas now appear.
After rage, all but her bones disappear.

Gazelles are roaming stars and bend a wind
That chills the eyes of creatures who are blind
To beauty we assign her in our verse.
Her wild florid looks wind the universe.
On this Earth we are each a fallen star
Who will become a sky star far too far.
Though mystics idealize her perfect shape,
The ballerina opts for swift escape.
She moves in beauty, dancing, eyes alive,
Playing, breeding, and prancing to survive.

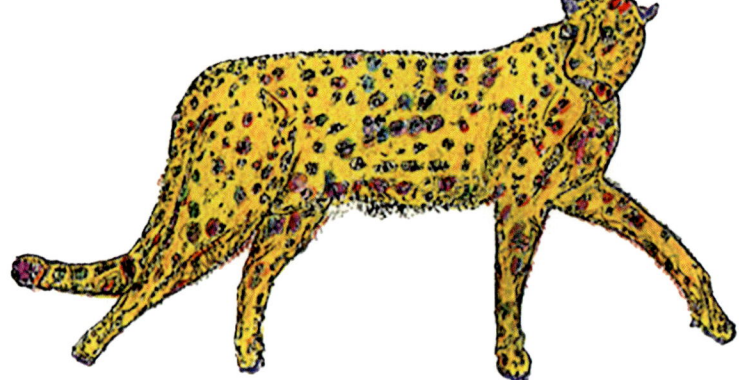

ZEBRA SUN & LION SUN

Punda milia
Equus greyi

Good morning, zebra Sun.
You graze the sea of sky,
Pee rain on us for fun.
Around our Globe you fly
To light another continent.
Your stripes of black and white
Warm us. You are content
To be the prancing prince in sight.

Meanwhile, the lion Sun
Crawls secret to your fold.
He howls. You group and run
Yet space breaks into gold
And blood. A few must die:
Souls to the lion sold.
Others grow plump and bold
And nibble the tasty sky.

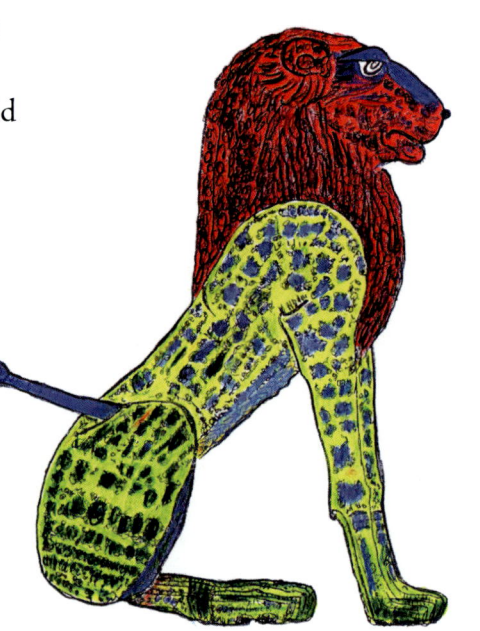

Our lesson for tonight:
Even a zebra in Sun
Cannot escape the run
Of lions when they fight.
While innocents must eat,
Hunters eat too. All bite.
Before the Sun takes flight,
Grazers are hunters' meat.

A CHEETAH MOON

A sleepy cheetah
In criminal night
Amid acacia trees
On the scrub Savanna stalks us
Below a black-blue Moon
Before the explosion
Of bestial daybreak.

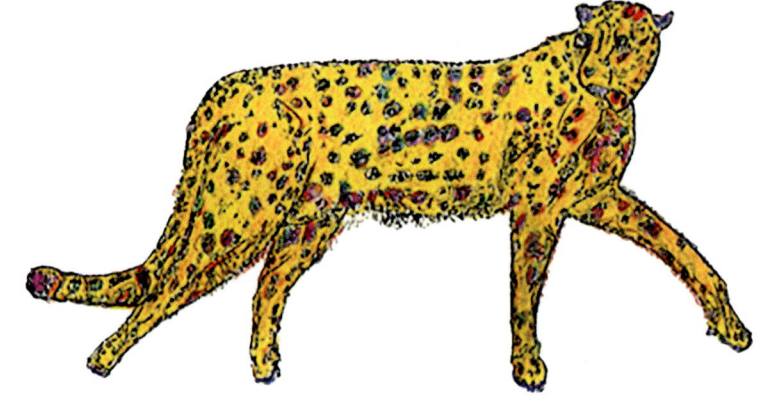

CHEETAH A HUNTING PAL OF EMPERORS

Duma / Acinonyx jubatus

In India and Persia, a hunting pal
    Of emperors and kings, the cheetah
Is a gawky string bean leopard who sails
    Like rockets on the globe, but, ah,
For all his speed he purrs and cannot roar
    And must eat swiftly what he kills,

Since as a lightweight he can never score
    If a big lion comes and feels
An appetite for his choked herbivore.
    Cheetahs are yellow with muted spots
To camouflage them when they want to snooze
    Or hunt. The nose sits on teardrop

Of fury, the spine is bendable like hose.
    Ancient Egypt reveres him as
Magnificent, and when you see him dash
    And choke a Thom gazelle, who has
Adidas running shoes himself, you cash
    In all your bets, since he'll win gold

In any match. An archaic type, he hit
    The road eleven million years ago
And hasn't changed his diet or his wit.
    I see him snoring by a tree
When kids awake the champ for autographs.
    Keen and with kind dexterity,

He holds a pen in his retractable claws.
    He signs, then asks for India teas,
Springs far, bounding on clouds as his trapeze
    And lands in Nirvana on his paws!
The cheetah, humans, and plants all adore
Buddha. So too do kings and gallant whores.

Louise Labé (c.1522-1566)

THORN TREE, SUN, MOON, OWL
AND LEOPARD LOUISE LABÉ

Homa ya mti
Acacia xanthophloea

By a gorgeous hunk
Of thorn tree,
Sun is setting near a drunk
Hungry

For-a-beer-flood
Of Moon. All dark.
Then the blood-
Lunar body fills the park.

Ancient Artemis soon
Commands the skies.
This bounding astronaut's Moon
Of minerals beautifies

Her Moonquake cratered lakes.
Our satellite (eternally lighted peaks) looks down
From her side and shakes
Earth's tides with a frown.

Then, concealed in a lunar chateau,
The African leopard moves in
Where his eyeballs glow
Like a bathtub of blazing gin.

HIPPOPOTOMUS

Kiboko
Hippopotamus amphibius

By day the hippo is submerged on river sand.
By night the tubby beast roams up to graze the land.
Stumpy legs and huge bulk, he's safe from predators
Except for man who wants his blubber and abhors
Him trampling crops. In Sun or lake, he basks a while
Though may attack small boats, thinking them a crocodile.
He seems to be a Disney prop, a bloated bull,
Tranquil, funny, benign, never caring to brawl.
Untrue. He's fast as shit on wheels, ready to kill,
And if you block his way you better take a pill
Since you're about to die! Sometimes, he's near your house,
Foraging your lawn. Neither villain nor a mouse,
The hippo will protect its calf, its path and food.
Gaze at this wonder & keep him in a gentle mood.

RHINOCEROS IS A BEAUTY

Faru
Diceros bicornis

The rhino is superb, a beauteous thing
        Among all animals.
In Nepal he's majestic like the king.
        The tyrant hunter all
In knightly armor, who each year shoots one tiger.
        In Africa the rhino's plain,
Solitary, black or white. He too is farmer
        In his own terrain,

Renewing earth while munching grass. He'll charge
        If you usurp his space.
I have stood silent by him, by his large
        Abundantly strange face.
Love him, his horn for which the Chinese kill
        For aphrodisiacs.
The rhino is superb, a beauteous thing,
        A loner animal

Standing beside a river or a spring,
        His meditation hall.
His only threat—extermination. Chill
        Out. Beauty won't attack.
His horn, a cutlass in bold ivory,
        Can make you climb a tree
In fear. But fear no veggie rhino. Fear the clap
        And tyrants, not this chap.

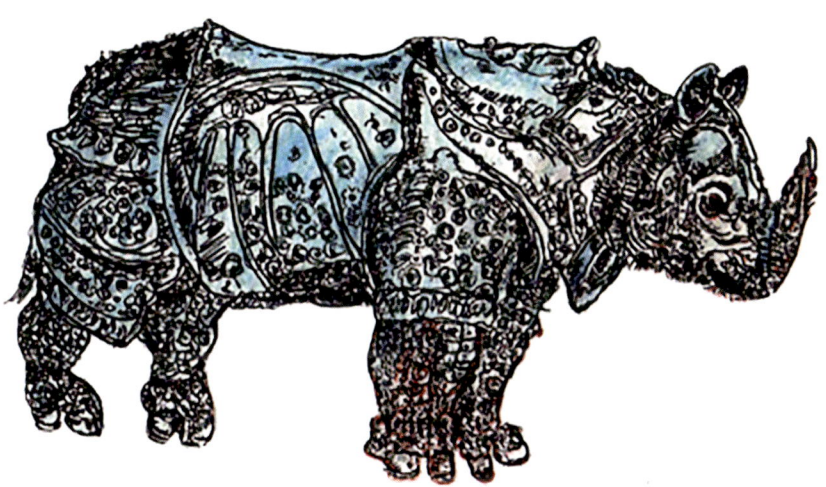

ELEPHANT, A MOUNTAIN WHO SELDOM GROANS

Tembo or Ndovu
Loxodonta Africana

When sacred elephants grow hot and mate,
They do not howl or stand upon their head,
But fusing back-to-back they copulate,
So, Theobald the Physiologus[2] said.

In modern times this animal lives just
One hundred years and not three centuries,
And when their loins are overcome with lust,
The bull climbs missionary high to please.

The schemes of elephants are memory wise,
Deeper than trunking grass into their sack.
When danger comes, they glare with tiny eyes
And squash the Lilliputians' vain attack!

These lumbering mountains very seldom groan.
Land Poseidons, they flatten jungle stars
And czar, cactus bloom and termite mound,
And on the march chew trees like candy bars.

Elephants have great visions, are slow plump
Professors rumbling from trunk to rump.
Often small white birds under their feet
Fly to their backs to peck an insect treat.

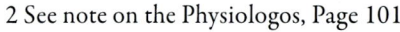

2 See note on the Physiologos, Page 101

ELEPHANT IN A LETHAL QUICKSAND BATH

Below Kilimanjaro in these wetlands
Is Paradise for wading in the mud
And water. Mammoths stand on massive hands,
Their pillar legs glimmer in stinking crud.

In a small pond an older elephant
Cools off and joys! Far off the green hills chant!
The local wind has settled on his black
Back mirroring with sun. But when this sack

Of nature's hugest beast begins to sink,
He struggles in the slippery swamp. In a wink
His ears float like wings. Only a hunched leg

And tusks are visible. Then beg-
ging air, his trunk shudders. Day beams fade.
And so the older elephant is shade.

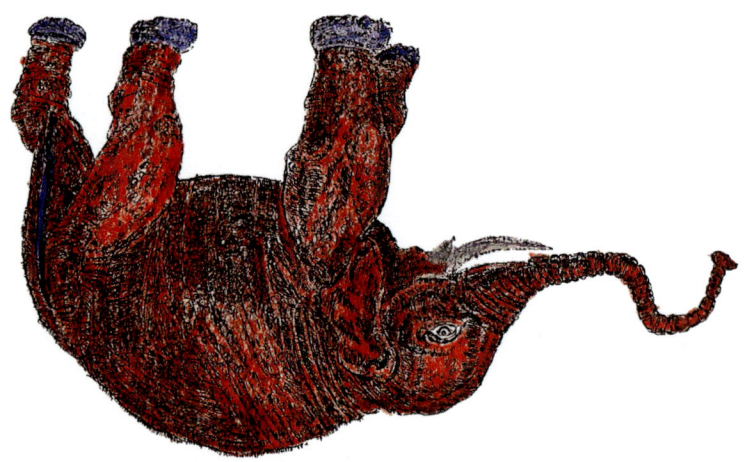

BUFFALO MOVE MEDITATING SLOW

Nyati
Syncerus caffer

Low morning buffalo
Move meditating slow
But unlike sister cows
These bovines freely browse.

Maasai build huts of mud
And dung, and mix the blood
Of bulls with milk to make
Yogurt milkshake.

Yet can't domesticate
The buffalo. Their fate
Is lumbering massive on
Savannas of the dawn.

Their eyes (big as huge balls)
Glower as ghostly halls
Of wisdom. Who can know
The loves of buffalo?

Their locomotive rods
Of steel become great gods.
Thirsty, fifty in a row
Line up, their bodies low,

Waiting for power water
To fend feline-teeth slaughter.

Though slow, the buffalo,
Like every animal.
Gobs of dark buffalo
Are soldiers on the go.

As they consume the plains
Their cosmic vision reigns.
Marching on Mars, each toe
Contains an astral glow.

CROCODILE SNAPS HIS TEETH TO SMILE

Mamba

Crocodilus niloticus

The crocodile is blue gray like the Nile.
A friendly chap, he snaps his teeth to smile.
The croc lies mouth wide open, yet not to breathe,
 But to let tiny insects cleanse his teeth.

By day the Sun transforms him into rock,
A prostrate worshiper, an armored sock,
A filigree of stone. At night to eat,
He arrows through the waters for his meat.

When crocodiles grow wings, they sleep on clouds
Which at a funeral they wear as shrouds.
When enamored they lie upon a date
And float in ecstasy as airborne freight.

In Africa the archaic crocodile
Suffers this doggerel and spoof with style.
Be like the croc, stoic and without fears
And swim in love one hundred twenty years.

FLAMINGO

Heroe Phoeniconaias minor

Flamingoes come in millions when they plate
A lake with necks coiled down
Into shallow waters for their food, or straight
They fly in pink-white gown

Of plumage — crosses painted on the sky,
Like a vision of Constantine
The Great who, once converted, tried to fry
New enemies. No sign

Of battle in their flashy ciconiform.
Their necks twist and embrace
In mating dance. They feed on diatoms,
Blue algae, invertebrates,

And owe their color pink to carotenoid
In muddy waters. In zoos
One supplements their diet, play Pink Floyd
So flamingos won't be blue.

In the Great Rift Valley (where the planet
Almost splits), the flamingo
Migrates, a Milky Way of pomegranates
Popping down on Lake Baringo.

When I walk near, grace wanders patiently.
I look over thermal springs
To see if they will fly. Then suddenly
A million smart souls are wings.

FLAMINGO IN FLIGHT

Birds are our earliest flying dinosaurs,
Scientists affirm. No teeth and beaked jaws,

They communicate in symphonic song,
Crooning back and forth as in ping pong.

They are beauty queens and the world
Responds happily as voyeurs, loving them whirled

By goofy gust, gale, and glow of lightning
Bursts. Like nearby stars, sometimes frightening,

They cruise around Earth, these gutsy voyagers
With strong helmets beneath their feathery furs.

Like Juliette and her feared larks, the flamingo aloft
Is racing magic like Las Vegas soft-

Touch gambling machines that soon fleece
You, but at least our bird leaves bright memories.

YELLOW-BILLED STORK IS CROOKED LIGHTNING

Korongo domo-njano,
Mycteri ibis

The yellow-billed stork
     Stands ungainly in water
With a crooked
     Lightning beak
Spearing small fish
     Whom he raises
Like Sanskrit letters
     Drifting up from
Ancient underwater
     Parchments that inform
The stork's mouth
     With tasty wisdom.

IBIS IN EGYPT IS THOTH

Kwarara Shingo-nyeusi
Threskiornis aethiopicus

In Egypt He Is Thoth, an Ibis Head on a body
        On a stand us Body
Or the full bird is god-judge of the dead,
        And inventor astronomy,

Magic, writing, and even our first word.
        No bird or beast can boast
Such aristocracy of thought as this bird
        Ibis wading on the coast

These days (no longer painted on tomb blocks),
        And her nobility
Compares in diamonds to the awkward walk
        Of storks beside the sea.

Here both compete for fish and surf insects.
        That ibis-headed man
As bird is sacred still. She counts stars, detects
        Each shadow on the sand

For precious food, and as a force for thought,
        She stands in meditation
Of what she was and is and how she ought
        To be in each mutation.

GENET CAT IS A DOTTED MONGOOSE

Kanu
Genetta enetta

The genet cat looks like a cat.
She stops by our table to chat
And feed. Looks like a cat but twice
As long. Panther-dotted like rolling dice,
This svelte and limber chap spins loose
(Looks like a cat, but kin to a mongoose)
Back to the bush, and flees unseen.
Looks like a cat. She's no feline.
The genet cat is *not* a cat.
She stops by our table to chat.
While I eat, she lies by my feet.
Then disappears. Soon she will meet
By the far wall an evening snake
And swallow him like chocolate cake.

WILD DOG IS PAINTED DOG

Mbwa mwitul
Yacon pictus

Painted dog is
From his Latin name.

In Africa he's called
The hunter,

Whose pelt seems
The leopard-spotted canine.

The wild dog carries
A baby dikdik

Dead in his mouth
Across the dust road.

His whole face
Squeezes, looking

For a safe place
For masticating

The fresh supper
Hanging from his teeth.

MOSQUITO IS A MALARIAL FLY

Mbu

Culicidae

The mosquito is a booming, lethal fly.
        Our enemy,
Leaving us limp. We shiver, burn, and die.
        His industry,

Malaria, is his weapon of dominion.
        With a sting
He infects blood. Wicked force. By world opinion:
        He's a bloody being.

He is to be despised, swot and poisoned.
        The scientist
Explores all recent lanes of medicine
        Against the horrorist,

Whose mirco-bombs explode.
        He tolls the pain
Of continents. The old and young lie stowed
        Below the rain-

Forest mangroves where this criminal
        Leaves his parasite
In flesh. Only a vaccine might
        Deceive the virus. But none.

Swamp fly, we are lost. Join the jackals
        Entombed with the night Pharaoh.
Child killer, freeze to death on snow-blue
        Giant, Kilimanjaro.

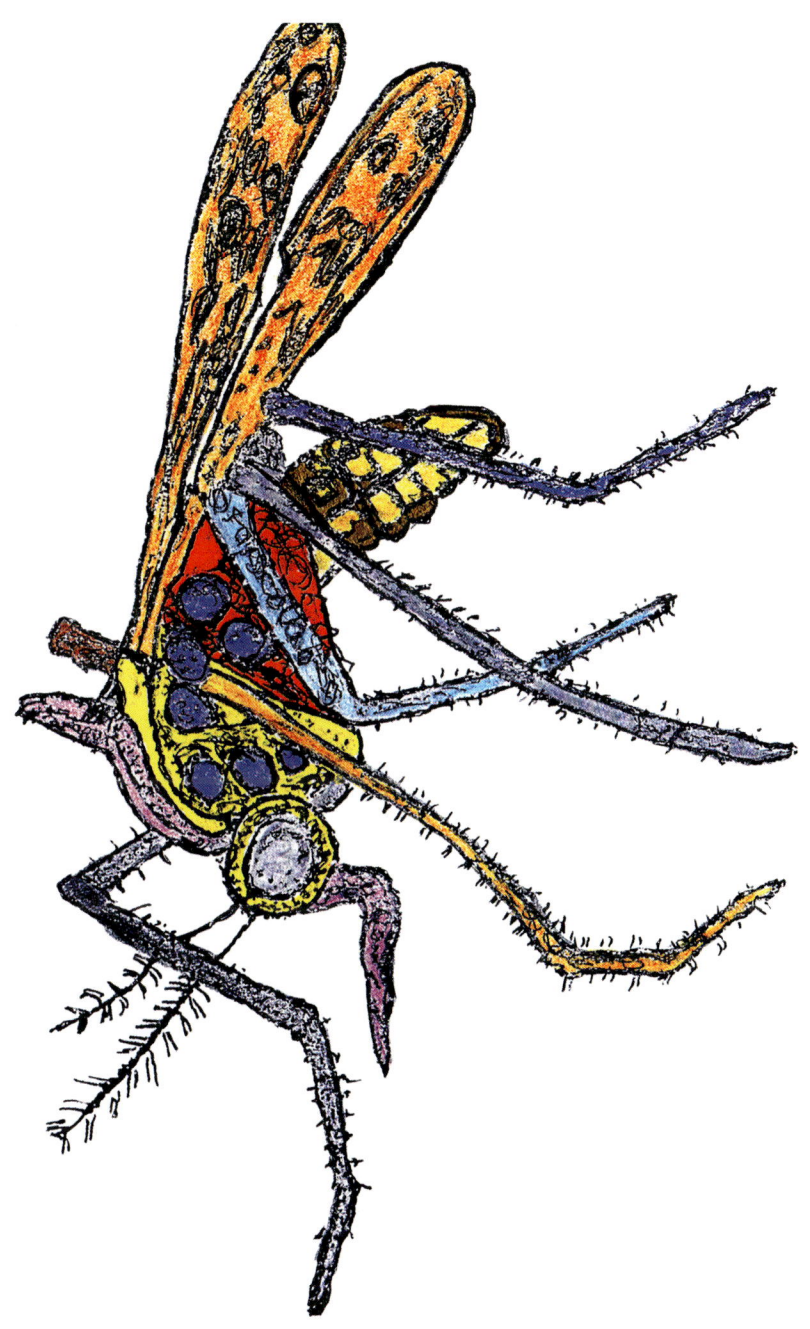

GOOD HUMAN BEASTS LEAVE EDEN TO KNOW

On the first morning of the Moon, in land
Under the birds of Ur, before the flood
Dirties the memory of a couple banned
From apples and the fatal fire of blood,
Adam and Eve walk in the ghetto park,
Circling a tree. They do not know the way
To make their bodies shiver in the spark
Of fusion, cannot read or talk, and they
Know night and noon, but not the enduring night
Of nights that has no noon. Adam and Eve,
Good beasts, living the morning of the globe,
Are blind, like us, to Apocalypse. They probe
The Sun, death-ray on the blue tree. Its light
Rages, illiterate, until they leave.

CHIMPANZEE SCREAMS IN TREES

Sokwe

Pan troglodytes

Chimps are our cousins screaming in the trees.
Swinging wild wingless and with no trapeze
Other than a high branch, their own high bar,
They whirl mad, frenzied like a falling star
And shoot back up in perfect form to claim
Olympic gold to French and Chinese shame.

In Kenya they race in the marathon
Of fun while humans still lace sneakers on
Or cartwheel down a hill like Bolshoi pros
Performing ballet stunts and without shoes.
Their habitat, like animals in all
Of Africa, is shrinking fast, their pail

Of freedom has but a few drops of water.
To save the few, they live in parks, banter
Behind electrified wire fences. Here,
Watching each other, who is the grand vizier?
Who is behind the fence? Surely not *me*.
Why can't we nimble bunch of beasts agree?

CHIMPANZEES BEHIND AN ELECTRIFIED FENCE

In Sweet Waters some orphans from Ruanda
Feed on fresh meat, nuts, grass, yellow banana,
Most of it thrown to them by the park ranger.
Proud, they're healthy now and roam without danger
In their wide cage of magnanimity
And show. Chimps seem to be felicity,

Grooming, eating, acrobating for fun,
But like their closest cousins in the sun,
Like us, they're fierce, tribal, and to survive,
If we go near them, they'll chew us up alive.
Even the rangers can't hop in their pen,
Since they are wild—not a tamed specimen—

Whose torso's five times stronger than a man.
In jungle trees they nod in silence when
At risk. They freeze while leopards loom below
Their branch, sniffing the wind and finally go.
The chimps are smarter than the animal
Who covets them for dinner. Tough luck, pal.

CHIMPANZEE AND CHICO MARX
AT THE ROXY THEATRE[3]

When I am ten my mother takes me to
The **ROXY THEATER** in New York. Once through
The film comes intermission and Chico Marx
Dressed bright Italian with a thousand sparks
And his companion chimp dressed up in fits
Of laughter, screeching, "Putting on the Ritz."
While Chico sings and dances fingers on
His piano with dexterity to con
All critics, Max, his able chimp sidekick
Plays a small red accordion as a trick
Musician, a bounding clown and worker child.
Chimp or homo sapiens in the wild?

---

3 It took years to realize that the chimp was surely a human dressed as a chimp,
   unperceived by most in the huge Roxy Theatre in Manhattan, NY, 1937.

BABOON, EXPERT IN FRIVOLITY

Nyani
Papio cynocephalus

If you're called *baboon*, you're a moron,
The name was made up by Comte de Buffon,
And even in Latin *cynocephalus*,
"Doghead" is not an admirable plus.

Baboons are experts in frivolity.
Riding bareback on her mom, a baby
Standing on a furry back hops slaphappy
To a first cousin in the family.

The family is key. Like the raccoon,
Bandit baboons are acrobats and lun-
atics. They're everywhere. Gangs steal the seed
Of newly planted fields, a troop to weed

Each fated grain of wheat as it were grass,
And soon the meadow's bare as their pale ass.
Their hairless comfort pad of flesh is typical
Of these forever jumpy animals

Who look for ways to creep into some cheap
Blimps filled with food and float off like balloons.
Now, all have conked out dreaming into sleep
Like wildflowers snoring under prairie Moons.

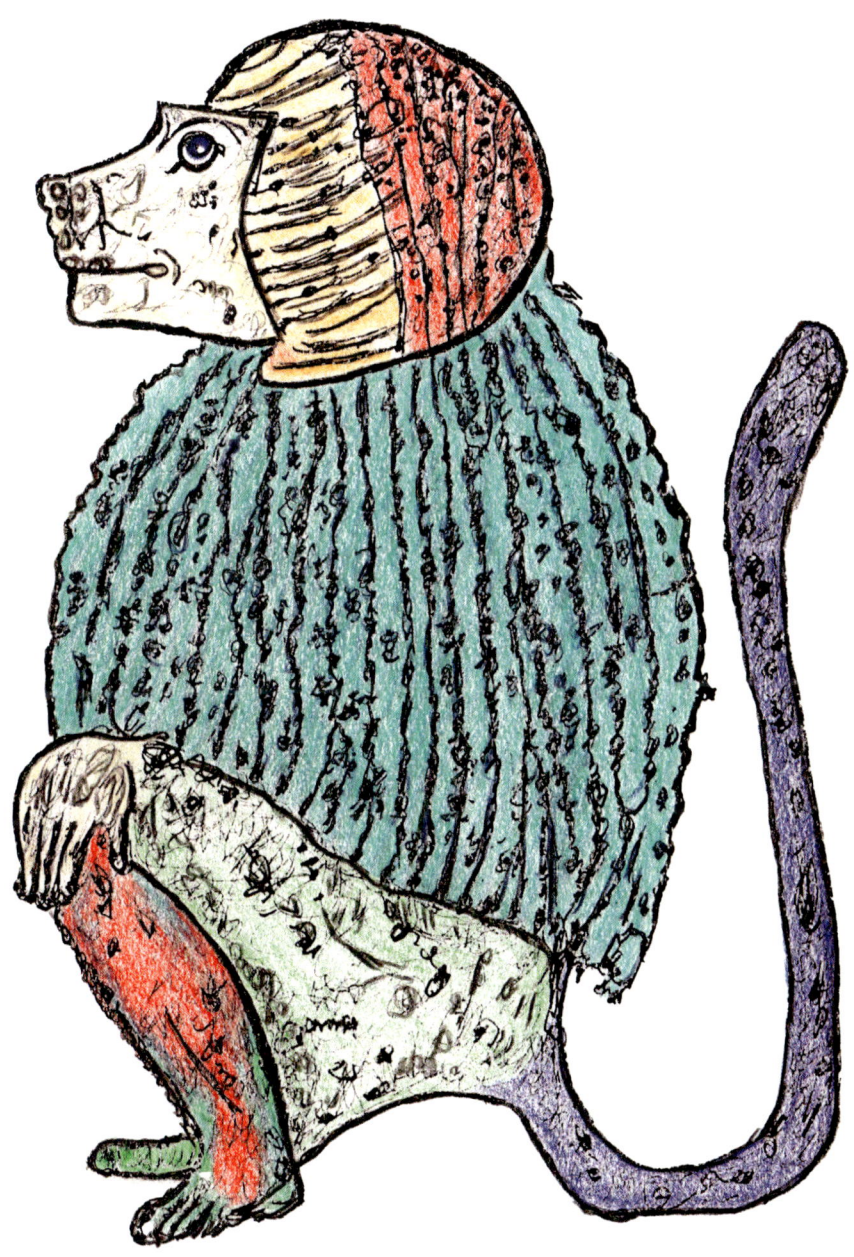

VERVET MONKEY, A LAUGHING THIEF

Tumbli

Cercopithecus ethiopsa

The Church freed François Villon from prison
For stabbing a priest. Jailed, he scribbles leaves
Of paper with irreverent chansons,
And *Le Grand Testament* in which he bonds
Both meditation and bold sin in one
Wild scam of bounding life. The bounding monde

Of monkeys follows Francois to the T.
The monkey's now jailed. Not for a knife
In a drunk's ribs, but for good looks. So we
Can see him swinging in a zoo. No strife.
In Africa we see nature's zoo from a van,
Catching a glimpse of monkey business through
A window or a lens. Each simian man
Or lady in the trees is free to chew.

Early one morning I'm wandering sole in
A tangle of drenched jungle trees. It's cool,
I eat romantic breakfast, though my skin
Is red with bites. A gang of vervets pool
Above. I'm there, they look at me and squeal.
I stand with a muffin box, not in elegy
For snows of yesteryear but dreaming real
Cheetahs and leopards racing for the kill

Of zebra and gazelle. And oops my hand
Is empty. A vervet's stealthy fingers strip
The muffins from my grasp. In the same band,
He excels like robber Villon. Without a slip,
He steals and in a flash scamps up a tree.
I look at him and my stolen warm buns
Dwell in his mouth. He looks down, screams at
Me. Laughs, thrills! He's scooped me on the run.

COLOBUS MONKEY GULPING SKY

Mega mweupe
Colobus absyssinicus

The busy colobus sits eating leaves,
Insects, and tree bark. He gurgles
With himself at full speed.

A love call hollows through the jungle.
An eclipse hopping from
Mountain to far mountain.

Shadows of black Sun
On a titanic wall tickle
The monkey's tongue.

Rainbows slide down
To the tree haven
Where two colobus lovers

Rendezvous and dance
On a fat overhead branch.
They sneeze, comb each other.

Breathe hard. Chunk down
Lobs of black Sky. Giggle in loud
Giddy racket. And make a family!!

OWL IS A HOOT

Babewana
Falconiformes

The owl is a hoot. The poet Edgar Allan Poe
　　　　Hears her nocturnal howl,
And gothic and ubiquitous he lets her crow
　　　　Bell through his verse. The owl

Is far-sighted and turns her telescopic eye
　　　　A hundred eighty degrees
So she can see her prey. She is the perfect spy.
　　　　In Zanzibar her species

Likes the rain forest. Is dense unlike the plain.
　　　　In sunlight almost blind,
At night she turns her head and spots you plain
　　　　And soon her beak or claw

Will crash into your neck. In Greece when
　　　　I am young, I hear the nightingale
And owl, a garden duet vying for their song
　　　　To reach a lover. I

Prefer to let this evening predator be heard So
　　　　Young squirts will sigh
And old farts recall, and not make her sin as absurd
　　　　Bigoted beast-tales do,

Calling up her Arabian nose and treachery.
　　　　She's wise and is Athena's friend
Companion. In this malarial forest, she cries.
　　　　To an unseen star she lends

Her passion, making its remote inhabitants
        Connect with us. That's more
Than even dreamer Poe could dream, whose bleak tales dance
        To the owl's nocturnal roar.

So, when we wish for small magnificence
        In body-weaponized colored steel,
Think of the jitterbug owl whose dance
        Glares at night—and sparkles genteel.

ALEXANDER THE GREAT'S OWL ON ANCIENT GREEK COINS

EGYPTIAN OWL

Is this ancient Egyptian owl a pagan
Beauty? Or a bird turned Christian?
Is she an Alexandrian Jew? Pain
And ecstasy fill the white and blue plain
Of her magnificent eyes No need
For glasses. Deep-blue pupils seed
A living telescope that lingers on
The laughing Dog Star. Never gone
From our memory, the owl now
Lives everywhere, screeching WoW!
At night she hunts, feeds, no bonnet
On her scalp. By day she writes a sonnet.
Odysseus discovers her. With electric ease
He carves a flashing green ship to joy the seas.

CATS

We all know cats.
Yes, they are brats,

Smart as a skunk,
Never a punk,

But a winner,
& ever a sinner,

Sweet to be with,
Ancient as myth

When Egyptians
Make cats prescriptions

For war and felicity,
A scratchy history

But like cinema end,
A beloved friend.

She wears a thief's black mask, guts,
Power. Never goes nuts.

Cats are real as teeth.
To her our love we bequeath.

COBRA SPITS SPELLS OF POISON!!

Fira /Swila (spitting cobra)
Elapid

Nothing is without art and beauty.
      So, ice Hell is Dante's masterpiece,
And murder and the wasted death of Romeo
      Induce rapture unlike slow peace.
But life is Hell enough. In praise of cobra,
      He keeps our ecosystems trim
By eating other snakes from Africa
      To Goa where—with Hindu whim—

They call him *Naja haja* and he dwells
      In rain forests with mosquitoes
Spilling malaria. King Cobra spits spells
      Of poison into eyes of foes,
Raps round their throat and chokes, and all for
      Art, he dances to the charmer's song
In India, though flutes don't sway his heart
      Since like all snakes he's deaf!! He's long,

Long as the longest shark. He sports a hood
      And puffs up when he wants to scare
A victim he will swallow. When his good
      Body swells up, he wears
A profile of a disappearing ghost. In his
      Ballooning form. Well fed,
Only the mongoose dares to be his host,
      And with one plunge, the cobra's dead.

SIGN WARNS, BEWARE OF COBRAS AND GENET CATS KILL COBRAS!

I am scared of cobras. Near the coast
    Of Kenya is a rocky boast

Of brush and trees on a high hill I wished
    To climb, but out of fear I quit

Halfway up, being no Indian mongoose
    To choke the snake in a quick noose

Of teeth. But had the cobra beauty fished
    Me from the sky I would be mud

Or something cobras dump when they are done
    With noshing and cool out in sun,

And you good reader, would be spared the blot
    And rot of this failed astronaut

Whose mangled body lying in the light
    So hyenas gobble with delight.

THE HYENA HAPPILY EATS UP REMNANTS OF DEAD COBRAS

WARTHOG IS THE IMAGINARY BEAST

Gwasi, mbango or ngiri
Phacochoerus aethiopicus

Even your name is ugly, as if eyes of mud
And excrement had fashioned you as blood
Of the grotesque. How wrong! Good hog with ties
To common pigs, when gods made you, their eyes
Were blindfolded. Yet you, hairy brown busts
Of faux sublime, ferocious with your tusks,
Two pairs out of your mouth spook all wild cats
Of prey. Your trot is slow across the flats.

One look at you, you're safe. No looking glass
Will call you cute like rabbits in the grass.
The enemy of grace, you invent sports
Of bachelor sex with your forbidding warts,
Defenses on your head against the thrusts
Of other males in mating fights. Your lusts
Are big, your housing poor. You dig into
Abandoned aardvark burrows. What you do

Is enter ass-end first and then burst out
Into the night, smashing foes with your snout.
All things considered, *Señor Oddity*,
In heaven you'll find sleep; on earth fungi
Roots, berries, eggs, and even a dead bird.
Your sight is poor, rich your survival word.
By day you scan to be no cheetah's feast.
By night you are the Imaginary Beast.

SALVATION SAMMY VS AIRPLANE BARBARIANS

Salvation Sammy loves and saves each animal.
No slouch, he is equipped with finest rocketry to fall

You who will be consumed by ants and cheetahs as in a microwave
Furnace. Your plane and weapons will not save

You from boiling nothingness. Toodle-loo, murderers!
Scream and rot in your finest animal furs

You pillaged on the holy Bush. We
Are many who support the animals. Be

It strong someday. For now, beasts fall and disappear
More and more. Old tale. When shall more good appear?

WARTHOG ALONE, BELOW THE MOUNTAINS, POSING FOR A HOLLYWOOD DOCUMENTARY

Horrifying and grave as Boris Karloff,
On the bush like a lonely giraffe,
The warthog pauses on a mound waiting for
A slow victim so he can soar
Like an eagle over the hapless chap
And drop down with huge teeth and eat
The slow-moving herbivore. Hot meat
Is his survival He glares at me. No treat
In mind. Nor danger. Few guns around
Then to floor the animals. Now the sound
Of guns, from bush or plane & sudden terror.
Then each of us was an enraptured explorer.
The warthog is grave as Boris Karloff
Glaring on the bush like a lonely giraffe.

HYENA, A LAUGHER WITH BIG JAWS

Kikuto kingubwa (spotted hyena)
Crocuta crocuta / Hyaena brunnea

Hyena is a name worse than Warthog
    For scavengers. Contemptible
In name and habit, hyenas are a Gog,
    The slurping blood of a dead animal.

Females are boss and more intelligent,
    Speedy with jaws of powered steel.
When the hyena laughs, beware, your scent
    May reach his nose. You better heel

It home. He kills Thomies and wildebeest.
    Dog-faced, because of long forelimbs
He arcs to Earth. When famished he may feast
    On tons of termites yet keeps slim.

Hyenas are the garbage guys, cleaning the bush.
    The striped ones scream like hooping dogs
And Aardwolves, both cousins. They love to rush
    In at night, those gorgeous rogues.

Their only watch dog is the owl, a masked
    Egyptian mummy who stares and sees
A chance to pick up meat scraps and bask
    In Moonlight until a star pees.

CARCASSES

When our sole globe is hot gas
    Jupiter and billionaires and angry poor,
The hungry and the fat, are mere pewter
    And slime lost in a river roar,
Those lovely beasts (carnivores too) will be
    A memory. While warm Earth still
Holds human survivors, soon we'll not see
    Wild beasts in Africa. They will

(Like fellow breeds in India and France,
    From New York to the Philippines)
Inhabit zoos. Others will leap and dance
    In tour parks guarded by marines.
Yet there is time. There is time. Time to change
    Our ways. If we hang on perhaps
We'll find a way to vacuum skies. The strange
    Savanna will find computer apps

In city blocks, but there will be a time
    To choose an Eden for our friends
The animals. Where? The South Pole? Sublime
    Might be to irrigate the ends
And bends of wastelands. No more Carcasses
    To bury. A true Eden? No.
But while Earth has some plains and terraces,
    For beasts we must let beauty glow.

FISH EAGLE LUNGES AT THE WRINKLED SEA

Kwazi

Fukombe Haliaeetus vocifer

Fish eagles choose a mate, pair off
    For life, and keep on adding stick
And mud, and in their palace scoff
    At lesser folk. A bailiwick

In Denmark would earn him scorn
    For cruelty as Ben Franklin's take
On the bald eagle who, he warns,
Is thief, a coward. and a rake,

Unworthy as the emblem for
    Our country, who kills kingbirds in
The sea. A lake, a tree on shore
    Is all this fisher needs to win

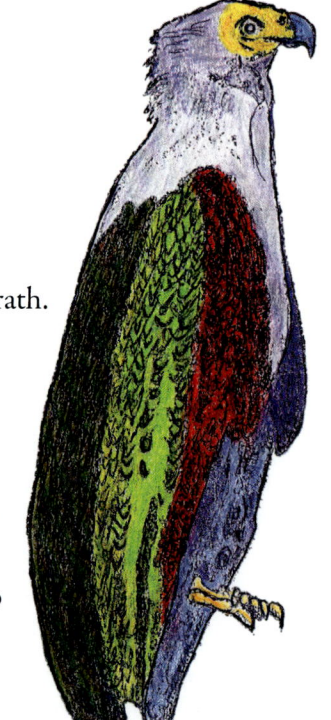

A plate of fish and chips. Forget
    The chips but keep Ben's words of wrath.
Fish eagles need to eat, but let's
    Not glorify the raptor's path.

The problem is profound. So be
    Decent to eagles in their winged job
Of lunging at the wrinkled sea.
    Though grazers eat and need not rob

A life, are peaceable and not
    Orgasmic for the sudden kill,
Visionary eagles love to spot
    Weak grazers for their breakfast thrill.

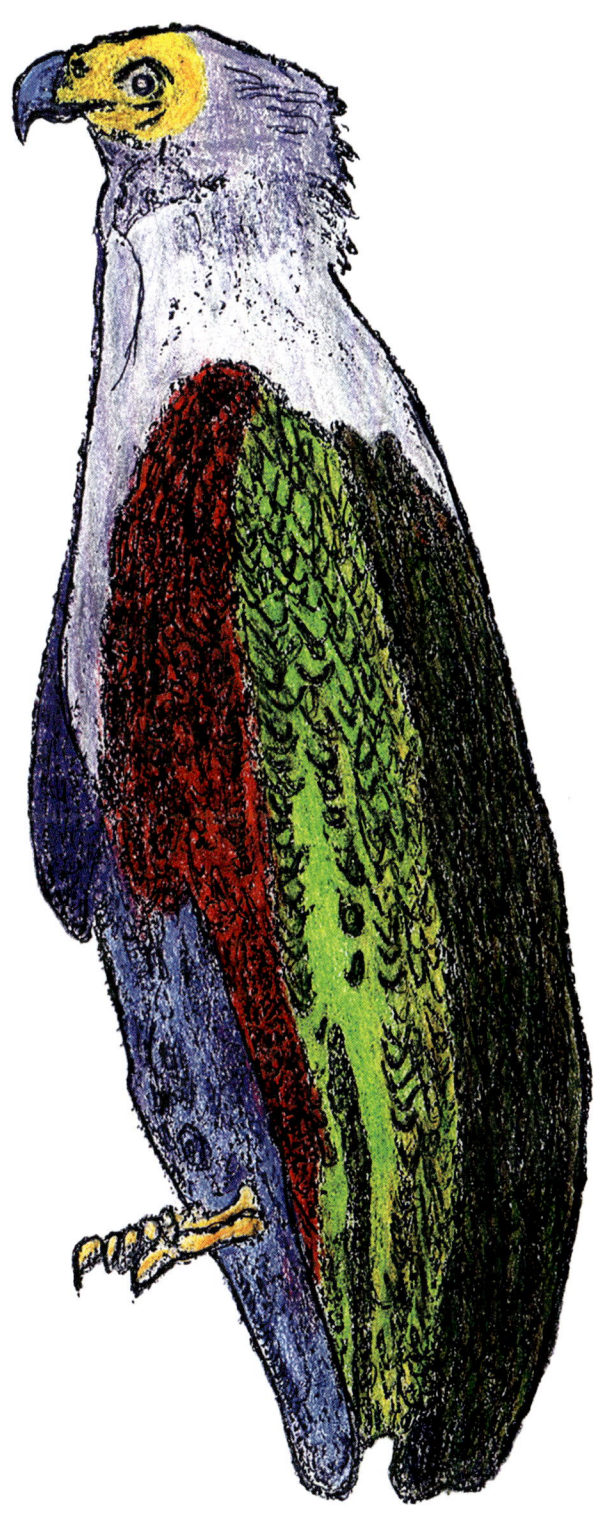

KILIMANJARO SMOKES LIKE
ANY OLD GREEK PEASANT

All morning Kili's mountain gods
Smoke clouds on a volcanic bench
Decorated with white pepper pods,
Smoke like any old Greek peasants
At their white marble table perched
Precariously on a mountain site.

All morning we and elephants
And giraffes who stand and sight
The far and meditate on clouds
Wonder when vast Kili will show,
Burn through her blanking changing shrouds
To let us see her crest of snow.

One frozen night in high Nepal
I couldn't sleep. We couldn't see
The mountain through the wall
Of darkness, yet we knew that she
Was there. At dawn the laughter
Of the gods, Annapurna, came

Enclosing all the sky with blur
Of white madness. I'm not the same
Since that lodge deck when I looked out.
At dawn-break. Kili finally burns her way
Into our eyes. Elephants about
To stoop and graze begin to sway.

Lions stop their hunt. The grand Sun,
The horizon's eye, cries KILI SHOWS!
Among our stars, Sun is the sole one
God among Gods to make Kili glow.
Our hot Earth scavenges Kili's snow,
Poaches his ice and vile heat grows

DOCTOR DAVID LIVINGSTON IN ZANZIBAR

Habari bahari, "Good morning, sea,"
Sad *Sea of Spice and Slave Routes* to maintain
The island Sultans in prosperity
Gained from cuisine and chained slaves sold to pain.

Once Africa's geographer lived here
And vanished. *Doctor Livingston, I presume,*
Are Stanley's words on finding the lost seer
Who's pleaded with the Parliament to doom

All trade of flesh. No win. The English queen
Did not. (No European or Arab ended
That plague. The doctor goes on mapping scene
And sources until disease finds him dead

In Ujiji. His dug-out heart is buried
Under a baobab tree. His corpse, carted by litter
To the coast. Sultan Farid orders him ferried
To Zanzibar where it sails on to Westminster.

Exotic Zanzibar, *Sea of the terrorized Blacks,*
Morbid slave ships where a black heart cracks,
Where Livingston gladly plans his trips
To jungle huts where courage shapes his lips.

Here's the scoop—a diseased doctor labors to treat
His patients—He can barely drag his feet.
 Then old Zanzibar grows rich on spice and raves
 About this wondrous nut of a doctor who saves.

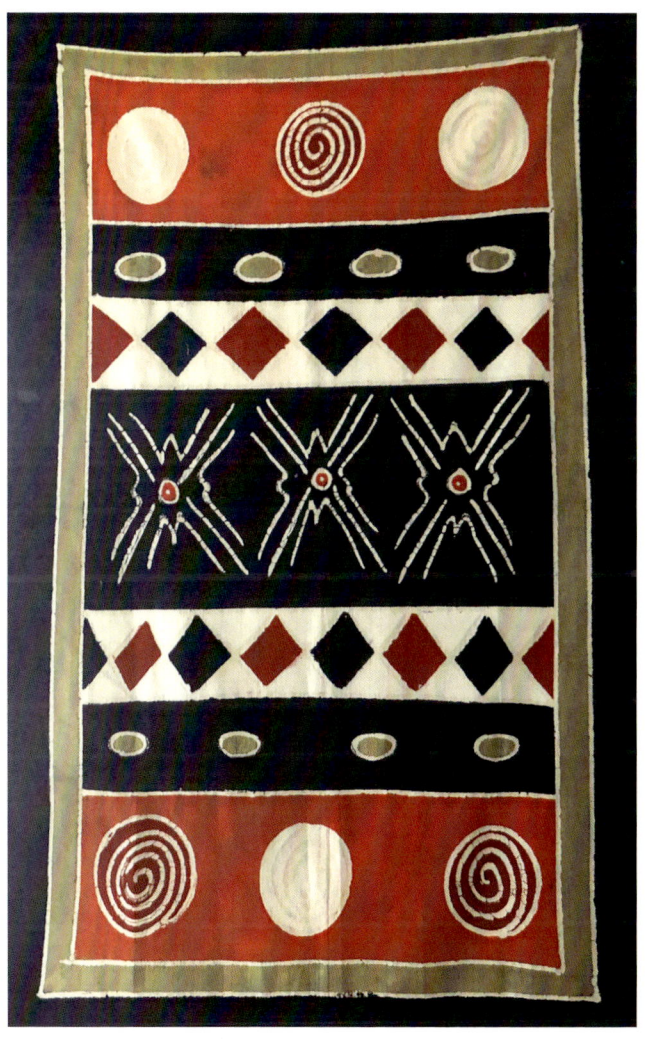

BOY SLAVE FOR SALE EVEN TODAY IN ZANZIBAR

homo sapiens

No other animal but the elephant
Whose tusks were ivory weighed like gold
Could bring what black flesh got in the Levant
Of Africa. In Zanzibar they sold
Black meat on platforms. Tippu Tip, named for
For his facial twitch, a grandson of a slave

And also son of a Swahili Arab, tore
The tusks off *loxodona* and led a wave
Of hominids in chains back to the coast.
They were not humans and no animal
In the grave slaughterhouse was like the ghost
Of bodies jammed down in black basement halls

In layers seven deep. They had no air.
Those who survived were jammed by Tippu Tip
Into his leaky dhows, shipped off like rare
Specimens in shackles. A pleasant trip
Till Tippu croaked malarial in his bed.
In Zanzibar, where the great *Routes of Spice,*

Slave, and Tusk kept glad merchants grossly fed
In seafront mansions where the vice
And center for exporting slaves had thrived,
The old majestic buildings now are packed
With fine antiques in marble rooms revived
As hotel suites for guests with golden tact

And hut or plaque is there. With turtles old
As ancient sharks, the Spice Islands' bright air
 Still reeks with trade of live black flesh for gold,
Clubs, guns, lines of chained ghosts and murder's tare.
Stone City stinks with trade of flesh for gold,
Of clubs, lines of chained ghosts and murder's glare.

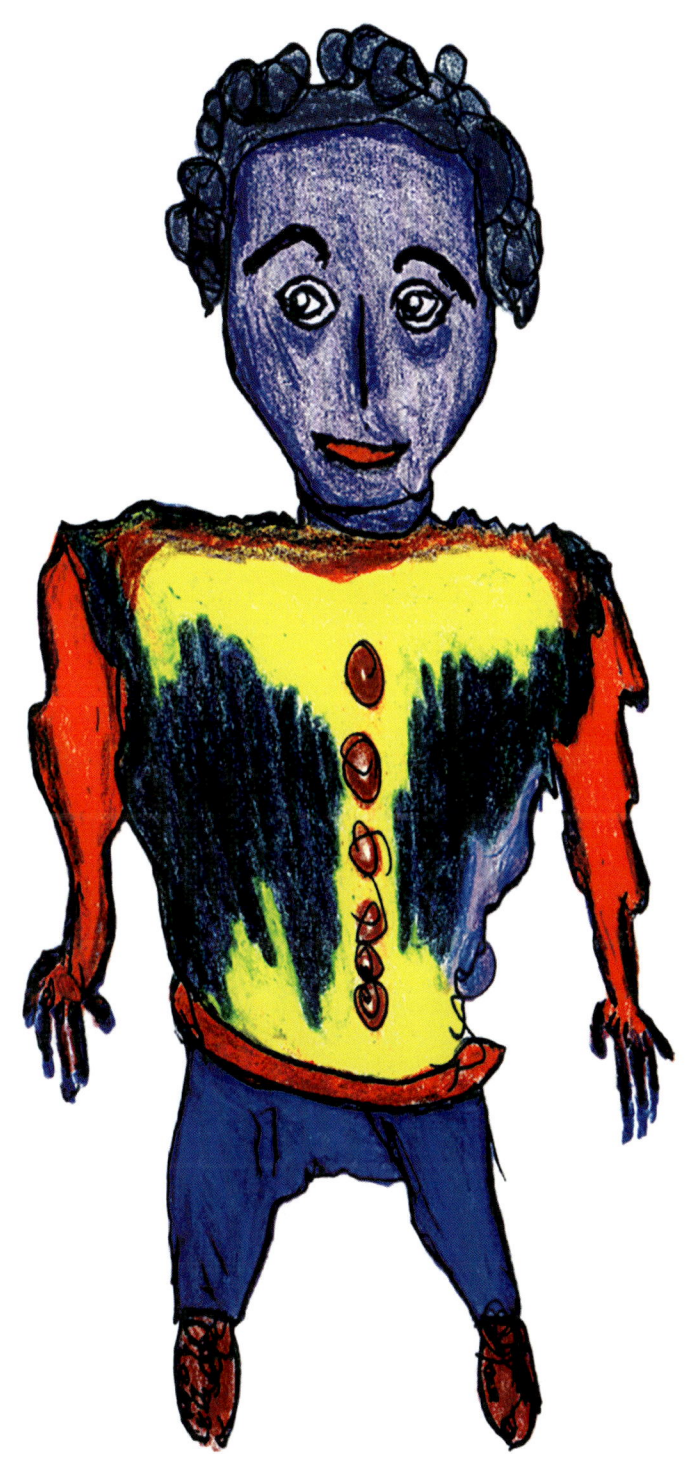

TERMITES DANCING ON ORANGE AND BLUE PYRAMID

Mchwa Isoptera
Amitermes meridionalise

Termites construct red and blue pyramids on the bush.
        They loom as monuments,
The work of small blind workers carting
        brush, dung, mud to build a fence
And mansion for their colony and Queen.
        The pyramids have holes
And parapets. It's Gaudí tuning in
        To desert art. Like moles

Industrious termites drill vast plains.
        They haul their loads in a short life
For the huge queen who is mother of all
        Her troops and stays the wife
And formidable commander till she dies.
        Then the vast colony
With all its castes of worker, soldier, spies
        Engaged in social duty

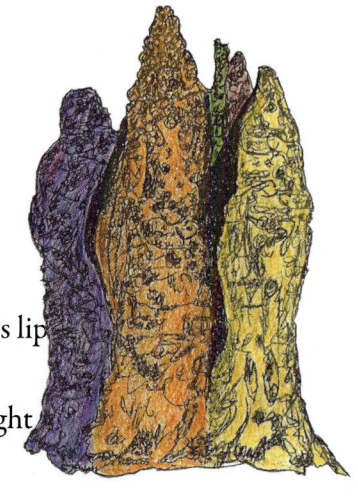

Becomes a Mayan statue on the plain.
        Alive the great queen bites shaped his lip
And eats, surrounded by small kings.
        Quite vain, she secretes from her bright
Anus a potent juice her workers drink,
        Their source of protozoans,
The Gatorade for athlete mites.
        Mites link their soul and life to mounds

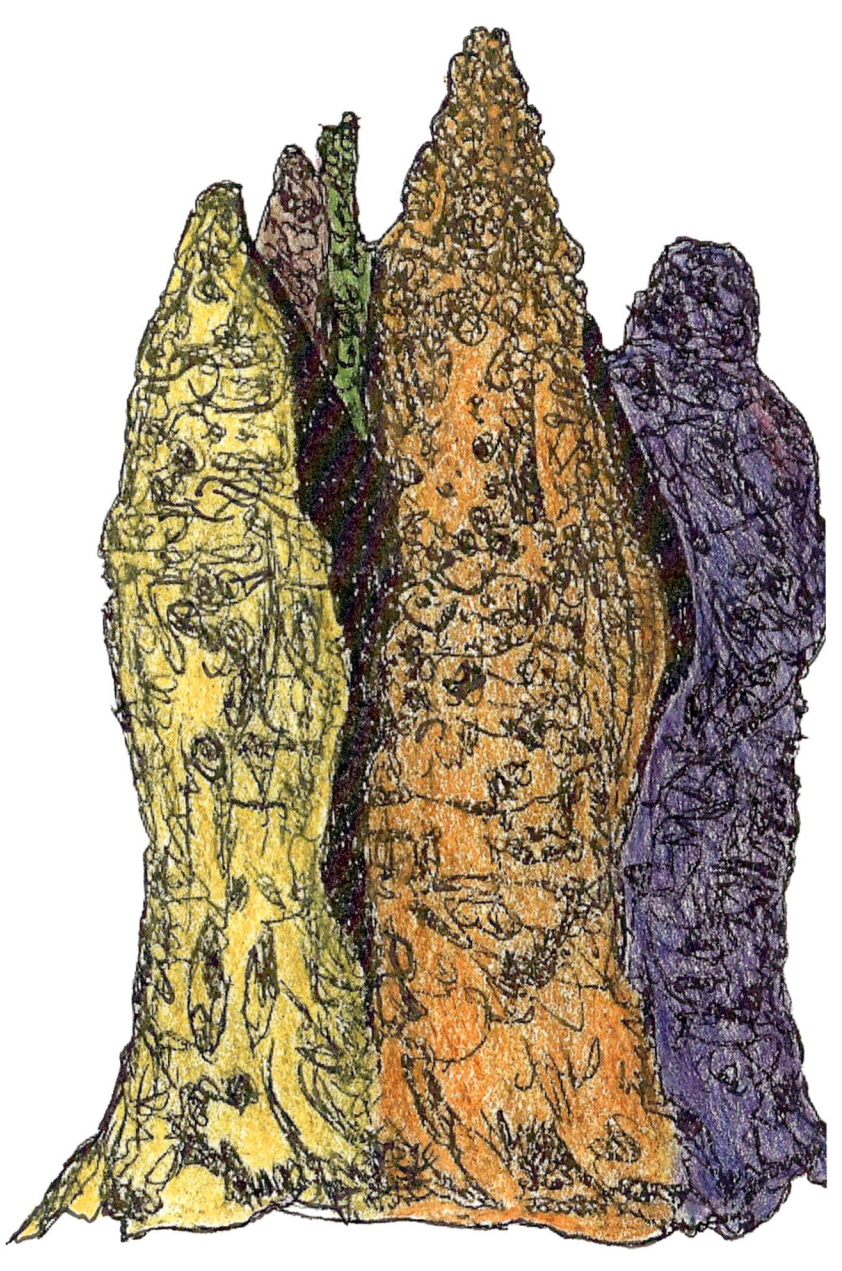

Of fungal gardens and airy tunneled walls,
        And guard their gallery
From all invading ants. Their mandibles
        Behead the enemy
With scissor blades. These wingless drones are feed
        Workers, a China of
The insect world, one quarter of all breeds
        Of cheap labor crawl above

The nest to work and cart provisions home.
        Well-armed, their skeletons
Outside their skin, the soldiers spit gas foam
        From frontal glands to poison
Fierce rivals who attack them as they march
        In strict formation to
Their work and wars. Touch them and your arch
        Of white-ant pain will do

You in. Termites dwell in a battleship,
        The favorite model site
For piety and church dictatorship
        And fire ants who bite.
In Africa the termite is the architect
        Of wonder. Genes balance
Castes, cannibalize old skins, and subtly perfect
        The rooms where termites dance.

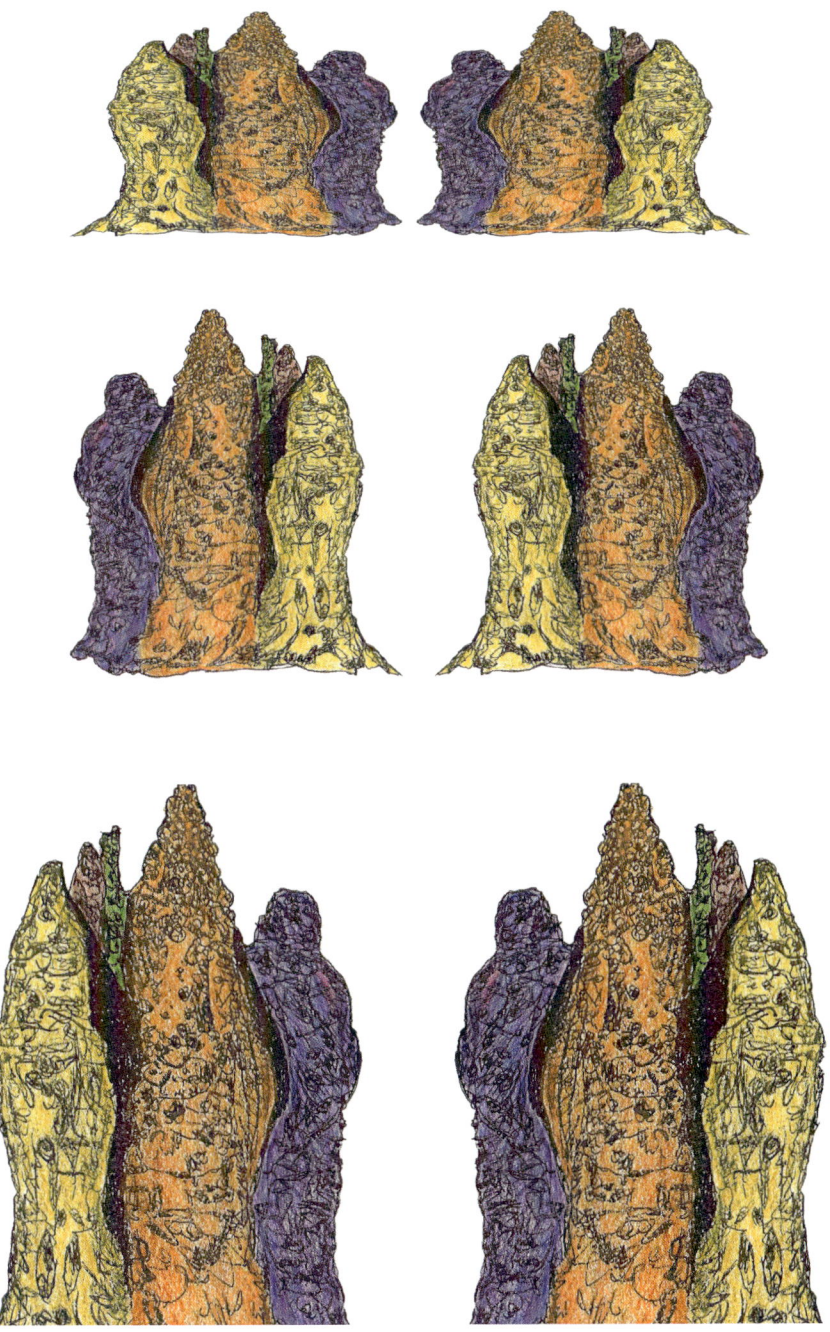

COLORED LIKE THE AFRICAN ANT PYRAMID, THIS PRE-COLUMBIAN MAYAN STATUE IN MEXICO'S YUCATÁN RAIN FOREST BLOOMS MAGESTICALLY ALONE AS IF FLOWN OVER THE OCEAN FOR AN UNHOLY BIAENNALE IN ITALY

As if from Egypt, the tallest Mayan holy pyramid
At Tikal celebrates the living and the dead.
It stands in the Guatemalan rain
Forest. Statues in Mexico's Yucatán also bulge the plain.
Slight-of-hand English sculptor Henry Moore
Imitates these vast figures. They soar
Into blue Anglo wind. He steals. With dwarf jungle always near,
Mayan green-stone parrots, falcons, and cougars appear
Like Egyptian hieroglyphs on the slate horizon,
Revealing rulers posturing for eternal dawn.
Though "primitive" pre-Columbian may feel African
Because of ancient similarities, can
We let into Africa this huge Mexican stone cousin from
The New World? Art steals. Do let the Mayan feel at home.

SPIDER, A WEAVER WITH EIGHT EYES

Buibui Buibui
Araneomorphae

Like Annie Albers at her loom,
The spider is the technocrat
Among the artists. In his room
His weave is fine and never fat,
Assuming every whim of space,
Including Da Vinci's secret frown.
Only a mirror knows his ways
Of spinning silk while upside down.
He plots a kill with his eighth eye
And eight quick legs. Then spots the fly.
As engineer of ancient fear,
While dreaming guts and a cold beer,
Spider lets a fly twist in his fine mesh.
Then dives and dines on her sweet flesh!

DANTE, SONGSTER ACHES FOR A WOMAN, CHAUCER INVENTS PLAIN SPEECH, & KEROUAC GOES ON A WILD VOYAGE RICH & COLORFUL LIKE AFRICAN WILD BIRDS

Dante writes in songing ink. The terza rima he took
From early Sicilian masters, who gave it to
Early Provençal in south of France. He scrawls a Book

Of Books to be chanted. At first, Jack Kerouac wrote
His *On the Road* in native Quebecois. He searched rill
And hill for a woman. Drunk, sweet, witty genius. Note

Dante's Nel mezzo del cammin gives Jack his On the Road[4]
Title. With Chaucer in his Tales, 3 poets made common speech
A hit. Their seas of words flowed and flowed.

Did these dudes find drama in African stores? Yes. Africa sings
Them. Even in Zanzibar (a slave trading epicenter),
Dante & Chaucer swoon in Swahili & Jack in English rings.

The glorious Italian love poem soaks in punishment
And revenge. A pity. In echoing verse of holy rapture,
For enemies Dante Alighieri craves torture and torment.

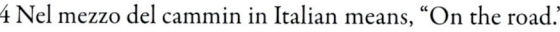

4 Nel mezzo del cammin in Italian means, "On the road."

GEOFFREY CHAUCER (CA. 1343—1400)

DANTE ALIGHIERI (1265—1321)

JACK KEROUAC (1922—1969)

WHALE, LION OF THE WAVES

Nyangumi Baelena
Whale

Mammoth of fish inhabiting the ocean waste
Is the whale. Sprawling on the tide the beast
Looks like a mountain or an island on the sea,
Which mariners imagine him to be.
When he is finished and desires to feed on fish,
He opens his great mouth and with a swish
Expels a breath tasting of flowery perfume
So he can lure the little fish to come.
Only the tiny ones (for those more fully grown
He cannot catch or even swallow down).

And these swim in his jaws before he gulps them all.
Unlike the fish who swallowed Jonah whole.
When summer flame and violent storms infect the air,
Muddying and troubling the ocean floor,
The monster shoots up to the surf and lies serene,
Where as a promontory he is seen.
Then sailors, tossed and driven, sight the peaceful form
And rope their ship to it against the storm.
They leap ashore and start a fire with some wood,
Warming themselves and heating up their food.
But when the monster feels the blaze he swiftly dives,
Sinking the ship, and robs them of their lives.

Now the Devil is huge body like the mammoth whale
And to some men he imparts his magic skill.
Throughout the world he petrifies the minds of men
And women, thirsts for all he can corrupt, and when
He finds the weak in faith he uses candied words—
Though by the strong in faith he is unheard.
He who confides his hope in him is coarsely heaved
Down into Hell and bitterly deceived.

by Bishop Theobaldus (11-13 c.)
Theobald's Latin Bestiary[5]

5 *The Bestiary of Bishop Theobaldus and the Natures of Twelve Animals (Physiologus Theobaldi Episcopi de naturis duodecim animalium)*, Translated by Willis Barnstone, Indiana University/Spiro Press, 1964; New Directions, 1999.

BAT WITH RADAR ECHOING AROUND THE PLANET

Popo
Chiroptera

His small Umbrella quaintly halved
Describing in the Airs
An Arc alike inscrutable
Elate Philosopher.
—Emily Dickinson

Bats fly from continent to continent.
Radar equipped they cruise by instrument,
Echoing around the planet. Winged rats
They are not loved. Twilight stealth bomber bats

Provoke bats in the belfry and scant joy.
Imagine dating a bat. Girl meets boy.
Before you know boy's in girl's hair. She calls
The vice patrol who call her nuts to fall

For a night bat or let him in her house
Unless he's Wagner singing *Fledermous.*
In Africa he's a bad god. I meet
Rain forest vampire bats. One hits my feet.

Must be dead-eyed or sick. The Moon comes out,
Lighting escape. I feel for him yet doubt
He wants my sympathy. He's not a raptor,
Prefers insects to me, hugs a black rafter

Or mangrove tree to sleep through boring day.
This agile monster grimly likes to play
But solely tropic flowers open to his tongue
So he can pollinate their love. Bats' dung—

Guano left in caves—farmers lay on plants,
But with one rabid love-bite comes the Dance
Of Death. Lord Bat, play a new isle tonight.
Let the London Queen banish the Bat Knight.

BAT-EARED FOX SURVIVING BIG TEETH IN AFRICA

Mbwehac masiko
Otocyon megalotisis

The African fox does not play games
For English hunting lords and dames
As they ride pleasuring their kill,
Nor chat with La Fontaine's blue skill
Whose flattering *renard* shoots the breeze
And tricks the crow to drop his cheese,

Or Aesop's bitching fox who gapes
At vines to steal and gets sour grapes.
From Arctic snow with heavy fur
To desert waste this small monsieur
With master ears and seven pounds
Slyly eludes the Kingsman hounds,

Bouncing on air since the Pleistocene.
Almost meat-free his juicy cuisine
Is fresh dung beetles or termites.
Out on a stroll on banquet nights
Like chefs inventing Chez Panisse,
It chows down fruit in gourmet peace

With spiders, lizards and a scorpion
Or two; then hides in dream oblivion
In bird-egg holes. He's beautiful,
Hunted by raptors, and yet full
Of Earthly wisdom to survive.
May the nose-pointed howl and thrive!

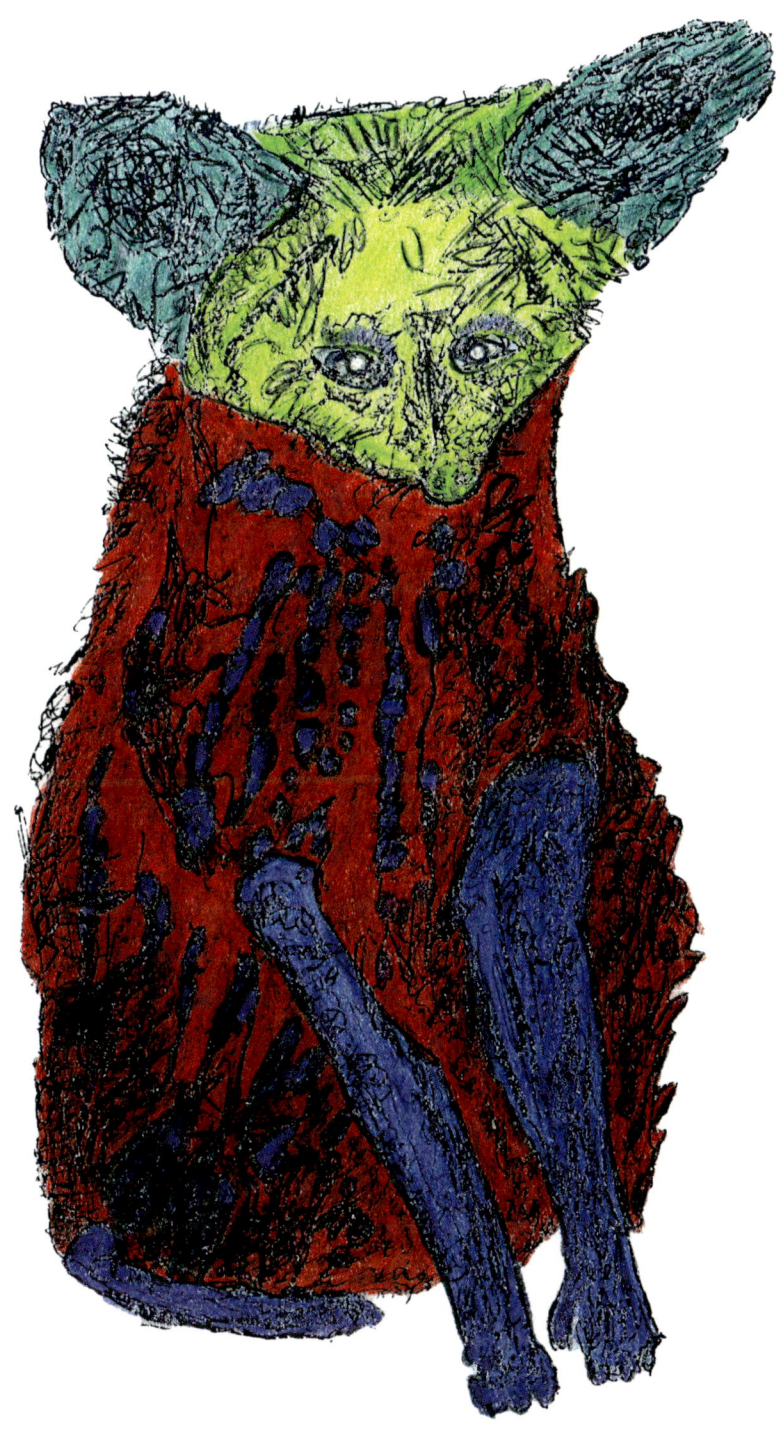

HERON IN THE RAIN FOREST

Tkoikoi
ardea cinerea

Chew a bunch

Of mbosen leaves

To get rid of boils

And timidity

But when the heron

A beauty bird

Fixes her

Eye on you

She will cure

Your brain and spirit

TORTOISE HAS AN ARCHAIC SMILE

Kobe

Testudinoidea

The tortoise like the elephant
Lives long. He seems to be a bore
And his archaic smile will chant
To you a hundred years or more

Of major eccentricities,
Sporting an exoskeleton:
Crustacean shell outside to please
The gals; an endoskeleton

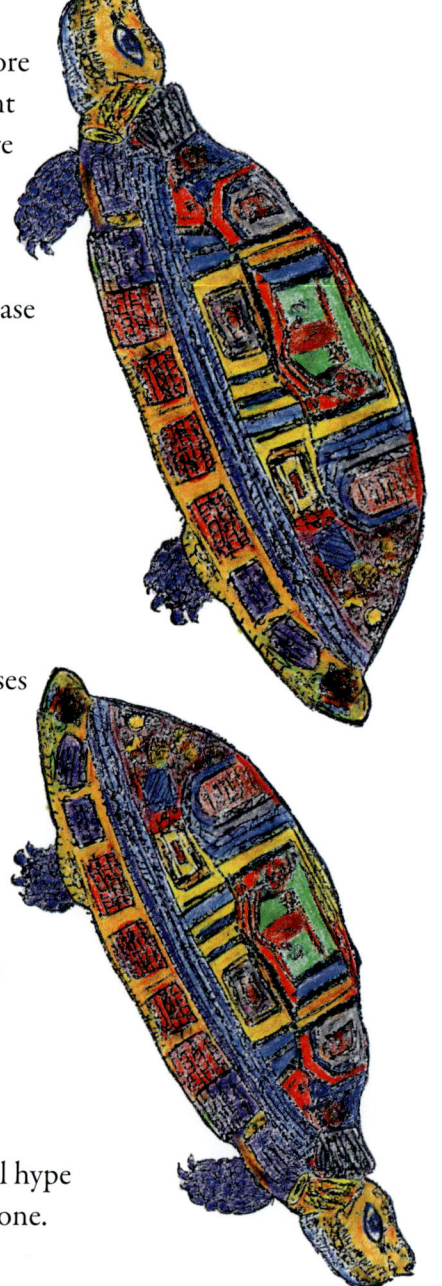

Spinal column set inside
Like normal vertebrates.
Don't mock the slow reptile
Who cannot hide being
So huge. Darwin took stock

Of him and proved that tortoises
And finches vary on each isle
Of the Galápagos. The mess
Of life on Earth is versatile

And logical. The tortoise was
His prize example of the shock
That tortoises in drag still buzz
Into the heart of every flock

Of those for Genesis alone
As the designer of each type.
You let time grind and spurn all hype
And survive in your house of bone.

TORTOISE ON PRISON ISLAND

The tortoises on Prison Island
Just off the coast of Zanzibar
(Miles from giraffes of Kenya highland)
Wear blotches on their backs, the scar

Of battles over women's lips.
I watch your prehistoric face
Eating bananas from the tips
Of my shy fingers with their trace
Of fear. Why fear? If I could last
A hundred fifty years like you,
I'd not be bored if I must fast

On bananas and morning dew.
A fellow mammal whale roams the Indian Sea,
Mouth open for fish to drift and soon not be.

OSTRICH WTH A NECK IN ALEXANDER CALDER'S MOBILE STEEL

Mbuni Struthio
camelus

Ostrich, you are a fabled being. You are the dream
      Of Marianne Moore and La Fontaine.
The other Moore, Henry, carved your fat rear in gleam-
      ing stone. Your bobbing neck is pen
And mobile steel of Alexander Calder who
      Placed you among his circus feats.

The Physiologos of Africa went through
      Your faults and virtues and will greet
You when you speed through Heaven as you zoom on land.
      You move three hundred pounds as fast
As cheetahs in their sudden burst when they command
      The plains to gain a raw repast.

Strange bird. You do not fly, but you have wings with claws.
      You do not hide your head in sand,
But do lie down and hide as mounds of Earth. One flaw,
      You can be mean, yet move in bands
With peaceful zebras. The odd couples. On two toes
      Alone you walk and run. Your smell

Is sharp, your eyes supreme and crooked
      Glows. You're killed for feather, meat, and pelt.
Except for farms, you roam only in Africa.
      And roaming you twist your neck
Like an old hose. You prance by lakes and the savanna.
      Don't dance with me. I'll be a wreck.

You raise your crooked neck to rivulets of mist
    Just as the Sun cracks through with dawn
And all deride you as absurd. When day has kiss
    The Earth, you males are sitting on
Fresh eggs, a noble chore, though you invoke black clouds
    And even God finds not a word

Of praise. In Job he says you're slothful, stupid, proud
    Of midget wings, impious bird
Whose only fame is running faster than a horse.
    Good ostrich, we look awkward too
But we can buy fine clothes, learn manners in a course.
    Keep your own sky of eyeball blue.

AHMED MBINDA, RANGER IN JOZANI RAIN FOREST WITH CROCODILE–FILLED SWAMPS & DINKY WOODEN BRIDGES

Malarial mosquitoes bite
You even in the Mosque

Or when jabbering in the street.
After your aunt's death,

You sleep outside
For three days of condolences.

Not the mosquito!
Clouds of them swarm

Buzzing round your head.
"Everyone gets malaria

Who lives here!" You claim,
"Even Christians get the bug!!"

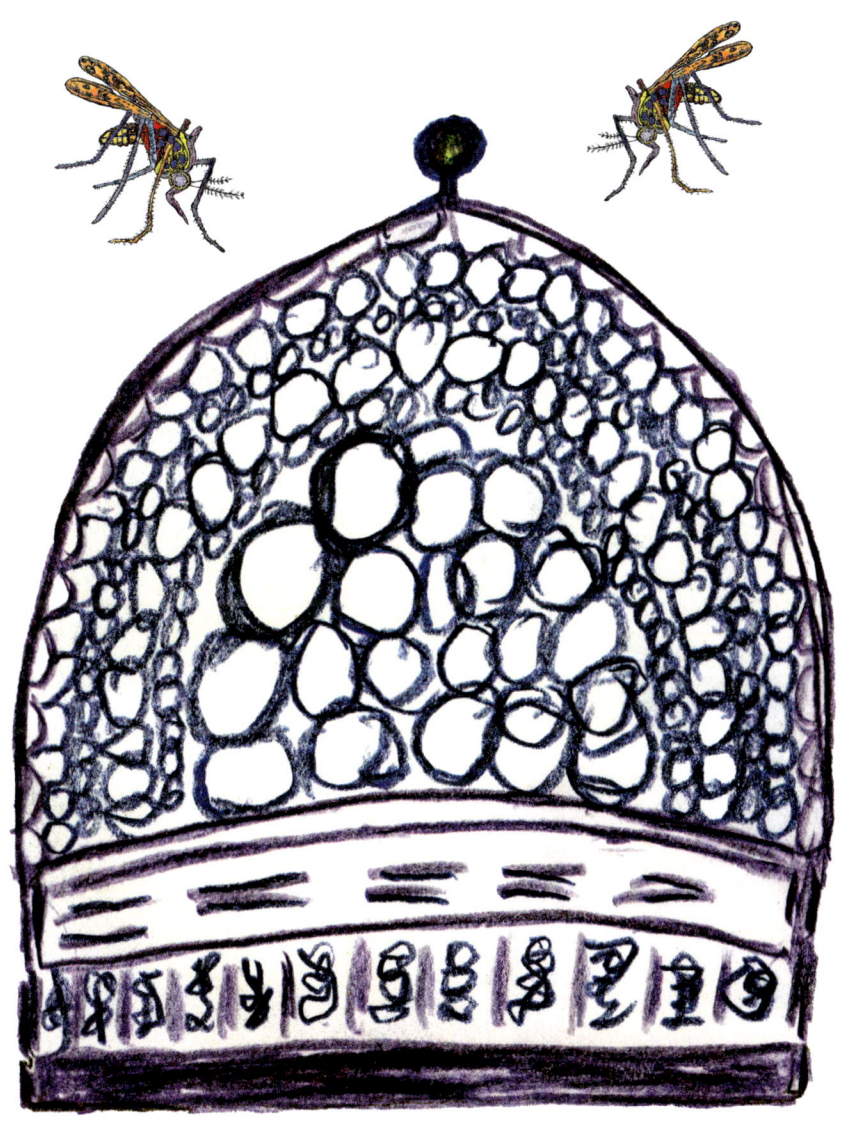

JACKAL THE NIGHTINGALE OF CANINES

Bweha

Canis aureus / Canis mesomelas

Now for the Naturalist, you're filthy scavengers
Who eat the leftovers from bigger predators,
But jackal, nightingale, and tiger of the dog
(The canine slot where sages keep you in their log),
You are, like crocodiles and beer, antiquity,
A tomb friend of the Pharaohs in nobility,

A god with a man's body and a jackal's head.
In Egypt as Anubis you embalm the dead,
And you are beautiful, nocturnal, with a smell
To kill an enemy. You hunt in pacts of Hell
To seize a victim, and to mark down territory
You spray urine and feces around your history.

Some call you cowardly. A lie. You even sing
At night, but worse than the hyena, just the ring
Of terror from your throat will make a zebra yelp.
Dozing by a bush you look fragile, needing help,
Help for the Pharaoh's mate. Yet how to intercede
When like coyotes and the wolf you interbreed

With dogs? Stay as you are. When lions and large cats
Have had their fill, please eat and prance around in spats
Matching your black-tipped tail. Black back or golden bright
Romantic dog, you hunt and haunt at dusk and night.
A slender wolf chomping gazelle and grasshopper.
Underground god, you serenade the dead up here.

CUCKOO WHOSE NOTE MAKES US FLOAT

Mtobo

Cuculidae

The Cuckoo is a bird   whose bell is heard When
her name is said.   Then a bell of lead
Becomes a sphere   of silver to the ear
And every tree   blooms like a dappled sea
Of fruit and mist   and every hill is kissed
With *cuckoo cuckoo*   and an echo too
Beautiful for song.   The cuckoo is not for long
In his love nest   but lays his eggs to rest
Each night with a   new love, then flits away.
I am surprised and pleased   to hear her seized
With tricks, content   on the first continent
With her own flock   of thorn trees.
Soon I'll dock   far from her thorn trees here.
I'm not forlorn.   How can one morn
When stars appear?   Never can she disappear
Or cease her cuckoo note   making me float!

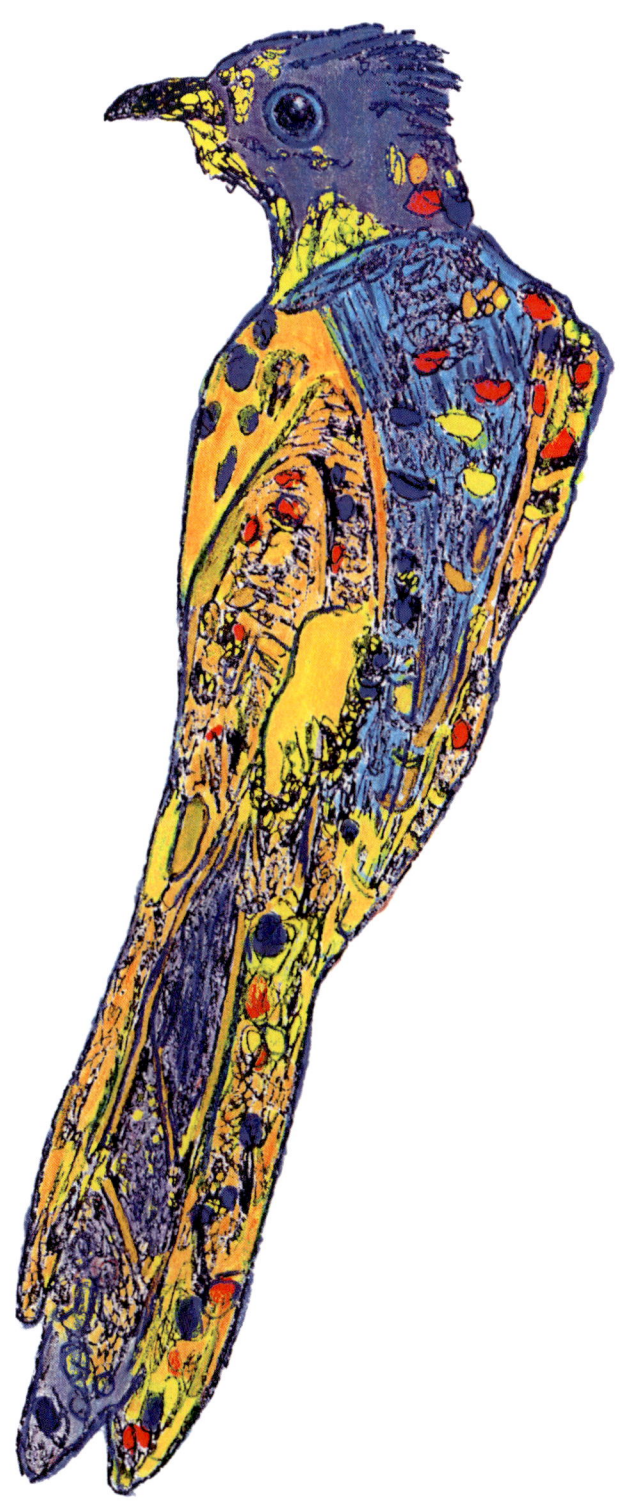

UNICORN (ORYX)

Here you have the beast that cannot be!
They didn't know it and it came by chance.
They loved its neck and wandering reverie,
The still light of its gaze, bearing, and trance.

Really, it never was. Yet since they loved it,
A pure beast came to being, and there was room
For it, always, and in that space it fit
Brightly and loose; it raised its head to whom

It wished. No need to be. They gave no corn
To it, yet nourished an idea it might
Exist, and the beast took on such power

From its forehead it grew a horn. One horn.
It came to a young virgin, came deep white,
Was in her silver mirror and in her.

Rainer Maria Rilke (1875-1926)

BLUE WILDEBEEST, HUNCHBACK OF THE SAVANNAH

Nnyumbu
Connochaetes taurinus

The great blue wildebeest, a hunchback of the plain,
      His shoulders higher than his rump,
Make him the awkward giant antelope of pain.
      He seems pleased. Never a grump
Who knows? He mutters and owns a pleasant brindled coat.
      In groups, though often solitary,

Dressed in gold mane and flowing tail, his willow throat
      Is almost covered by his fairy
Green beard. The fable of his year is the migration,
      South Africa to the frontier
Uganda, and a million-mammal celebration
      Commanded by an inner seer

To seek new grazing land. In this transcendent march
      They dig a highway Roman-hard,
Designed by engineers who might invent an arch,
      But here it is a highway starred
Like a Great Wall of China made for leveling ground
      And grass. Alone, the *gnu*, his name

In Kjoikhoi, may race off terrified and prance
      And wheel about, throw up his heels,
And gaze at compass points in an erratic dance.
      He has these fits, this beast of steel.
His massive horns must logically send utmost fear
      To predators. Sometimes he'll
Stand and stare them down. When he stampedes, you'll hear
      His gnu's cosmic throat. Maybe
It's *wrong to judge this most abun*dant sight, and love
      What you can't figure but can't forget.

WHITE UNICORN IN AFRICA, ASIA, AND LE MUSÉE DE CLUNY IN PARIS

Many have written of the unicorn
From Pliny to Rilke. Then back to wise
Confucius immeasurably forlorn

On hearing the unicorn is slain. His eyes
Mourn the fallen beast. Emperor Genghis Khan
About to invade India meets a horse

With deer body and a white horn, who bans
Calamity: "Forgo your bloody course."
This imaginary beast of continents

Duels with warlords with his horn of peace.
Like moody gods and poetry, he vents
His anger yet soars high like winter geese.

Psalm 22 sings, "Save us from the time
Of unicorns." On Africa's savanna
The oryx profile spellbinds like Nirvana.

Now our beast wanders like a hungry rhyme.
The white unicorn in China is Qilin.
Silent as a giraffe he walks on clouds to win

A Paris virgin. She takes him to her lap.
In amazed tapestry her loved becomes his trap.
This imaginary beast of continents

Duels with warlords with his horn of peace.
Like moody gods and poetry, he vents
His anger yet soars high like winter geese.
Horrible gift. We're in an evil hour.

SONNET ON ANIMAL BEAUTY
& ITS ANNIHILATION BY HUNTERS

Every animal is beautiful
From red hyena to a full-
Horned sable antelope. Jefferson
Speaks of a more perfect union.
Now, his words apply to beasts,
Not humans. A human feasts,
Alas, on ravaging Earth. Not so
For the roaming figures who know
How to survive on the savanna,
Yet thug hunters from Alabama
To a Spanish king—who shoots
Animal for adventure; he boots
A hero beast for a horror feast.

SONNET ON IMPORTANCE OF
THIS BOOK TO ME & TO YOU

Painting and writing this book
Enables you and me to look
And live with animals who
Cannot read, and permit a blue
And white wattled crane not to stoop
But hit the road in verse & elope
To serenity and dream of peace
That may at least rescue a piece
Of Africa and let it thrive
In Paradise. You dream, but I've
Electric faith that a miracle
Of-who-knows-what? may halt the kill
Of beauty from our Globe. We need
Dream and hope so big beasts will read!

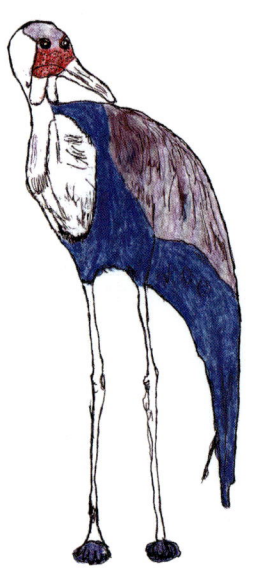

KINGFISHER OR HALCYON, SEABIRD FOR MARINERS OFF ZANZIBAR OR ALMOST EVERYWHERE

Dete

Halcyan

The kingfisher is a seabird who brings up her young
      Along the shore and lays
Her eggs in sand around midwinter. With her
      Tongue she cleans them every day.
She flies them off to homicidal seas and
      Waves cracking against the coast
And tests her chicks seized in the rage of spume, and
      Saves them from the uttermost

Destruction. But the tempest dies and lets her
      Shine, in the calm hatch eggs
Again in seven days. This bird's a magic mine
      Of knowledge sailors beg
To keep so they can sail in halcyon days. So
      Their grip of winter solstice storm
Will wither into gentle calm and spare their
      Ship, turning ice oceans warm.

These bestiary words are pleasing thoughts of
      Old Physiologos, and passed
From hand to hand. As the halcyon, she's the same
      Mold on Lake Nakuru. Off Crest
Regal, her chest is seaman blue and waits
      Alone in trees or tall on rocks,
And when she spies a tiny fish, her beak is stone
      Crashing into sea worms, reptiles, snails, and fish.

All possible to eat. Her bulky body is stuffed
　　　She always leaves a seafood dish
For her chunky chicks on easy street.
　　　Kingfisher or halcyon is one. All seas her range.
Sweet names From Nairobi, London, Shanghai, Crete

　　　May in centuries change,
But after grave tempest, halcyon days always return.
　　　For the kingfisher sailors yearn!

GUINEA FOWL IN A CONSPIRACY OF LIONS AND WILDEBEESTS

Kanga
Numida meleagris

An arrogant lion
In yellow grass
Naps in the morning,
Eyes almost open.
Guinea fowl walk.

The lion gets up,
Thinking about crooked
Wildebeests and zebras.
Suddenly all glare.
Males are walking past

Females in the grass.
Some guinea birds walk
In indignant formation,
Screeching. Guinea fowl
Toddle by the fury lion.

Painted zebra sniff heavy
Mutilating air And disappear.
Blue wildebeests occupied
With macho entertainment
Are bashing horns.

WEIRD LION TAMER

On the Kenya savanna
I meander into
A pride of marching lions.
Have stomachache.
Cannon a vulgar fart
At the Lion King
Who roars back.
Gleeful victory!
Then, I inch away,
Savoring the deep drum
Roar of furious felines.

DIKDIK MAGNIFICENT SMALL FRY

dika madoqua

The dikdik is the smallest antelope
    No bigger that a fat tomcat,
Precious as the creation of small hope.
    When teeth are eager to make splat
Of you, alarmed, you swerve, dive and leap
    From jaws of carnivores
So, you won't be a quick quick tidbit heap
    Of tiny bones for a wild boar
Or cheetah in need of antipasto. You
    Are grace on paws, a ballet child
Among the pros, and as the Child you Too
    Are Father of us in the wild.

WILLIAM BLAKE'S THE FLY

Little fly,
Thy summer's play
My thoughtless hand
Has brushed away.

Am not I
A fly like thee?
Or art not thou
A man like me?

For I dance
And drink and sing,
Till some blind hand
Shall brush my wing.

If thought is life
And strength and breath,
And the want
Of thought is death,

Then am I
A happy fly,
If I live,
Or if I die.

WILLIAM BLAKE (1757-1827)

FLY

nzi

Musca domestica

I
Am a
Dog of the skies
And food
To

A
Spider.
Even
Unseen
I buzz
In

A
Non-space
Of boring time.
Kill me
Or

Be
A friend. I
Multiply
Like a
Plot

Of Poison
Ivy.
My 6 legs
Crawl your
Dream

Deep
Like oil
In a crankcase.
I stick
My

Noise
In your
Far small nerves.

Blake
Has good
Glass ear, break up
Innocent words
For keep-
ing

Me
Alive
And yogis try
Not to
Wipe

Me
Out. All
Life is holy,
Even
Mine.

So
I am
Existence. Me
Too, I
Say.

I
Sip snot, am
Fire at dawn
And fly
Each

Day
To prick
A young girl's
Nose when she
Dies,

Try
To swat me,
I survive. A spinning bore,
No glamor
Or finesse

I
Am no painted parrot.
Dull me, Acrobat
of evasion I test
Pilot
For grand
Antoine.

But
On the insect
Globe, I am the Cat

With 7 Lives. Flee?
Not me

ANTOINE DE SAINT-EXUPÉRY (1900-1944)

Author of *The Little Prince*, most popular book in world
After the Bible. In it on a child's finger our Globe is uncurled.

BLUE BUTTERFLY, ORCHID OF THE SKY

Kipepeo
Lepidoptera

Butterfly, orchid of the sky and atmosphere
    Over what's left of Earth,
You are the universal Whitman ragtime cheer,
    Wherever you find birth.

The lepidopterists say in your brief life once
    You were a gross cocoon
And caterpillar. Writers like Nabokov lunch
    And dine on you, a spoon

Of fun amid a multilingual life of roam-
    ing like a butterfly is neat.
With many names, you wander a Maasai home
    Of goggling eyes. You float beauty meat

As an air insect. Be it Greek or Swahili, you pollinate
    as you hop from fleurette
To plant. With floating kin, you mate in flight
    And dress a plain in heat

With filigree of might. While most of your one day
    Is hunting, feeding, you paint land and seas
With beauty's hand, and find the way
    O butterfly, In Paradise, to pop free
And tame and beautify antiquity.

RED OR BLUE BUTTERFLY

Over blue and red mountains in Tibet,
Or flourishing in Kenya, dodging time's bayonet,

You are a cloud of freedom, delightful
Insect. You have just a day to soul.

Red or blue butterfly, we talk ourselves dumb. O
Red Land, what a treat on this rough meadow

To see temples in the air! Old farmers love
To make noise here, listen to a dove,

And make wristlets with a painted butterfly
Hovering over a noisy market. Joy's spy!

PEACOCK

Dausi
Afropavo congensis

The peacock is the Sun King of the birds,
Louis Quatorze but in captivity,
With no poor workers leaping to his words.
His feathered splendor glows for fans to see.
He is the pet of beauty on a farm,
Not in the bush for hunters or wild teeth.
His arrogance is slow and does no harm
To subjects since he has none. His wreath
Of poetry amuses a wishful Yeats.
Deep in the Congo, formed by nature's eye
Green like his train, and when he lifts his tail
To mate, he grows enormous like a whale.
This pheasant, no way peasant, struts and eats
Until his owner pines for peacock pie!

GENIAL TIGER

Chui-Milla
Panthera tigris

The panther, lion, tiger, and jaguar
Are cousins spread across two continents.
Now a tiger speckles hills in Tiger's Canyon
In East Africa. There, this isolated tree
Of muscle is like a lordly rumbling lion.
An acrobatic hunter with shrewd paws,
He dances on the hills to spot a deer.
A lamb or zebra soon will disappear.

If near his incisor teeth, you better run.
His dream scene is to leap and bite the sun.
Not mere thugs, tigers are smart,
Who measure stars before they drop in sleep.
This African likes valley, pond, and a blue
Cloud, and won't be imprisoned in a zoo.
To know his art, study Henri Rousseau
Who paints him. They both play a violin.

COMEDIAN PARROT

Kasuku
Psittaciform

A comedian parrot schools her chat
At the Comédie Française
Where her words echo out to fat
Mount Everest who says
She is his Grand Lady. Wallace Stevens ate
His precious imported sweets with her

After he came home from his gray
Slate in Hartford. Hear him compare
Her mockery bouncing from hill to hill
To Pliny the Elder. How
Does she sing like Lady Caruso, yet chill
Her skeptics? Better than a cow

In language skill, her windpipe (The trachea) shapes
Her song, and on a tree canopy she swipes
Her melodies from gracious Aurora. Before long
She goes to school with me at the Sorbonne.
I am a klutz who drops out, but she

Learns laughter from Henri Bergson,
Philosopher. In Africa she and a honeybee dine
In breeze. The Greek Wind Tower is her furred
Echo Chamber. Colorful bird,
While pet smugglers smash your habitat, you go
Off to chant on a star in your own chateau.

FROM *JUBILATE AGNO* (REJOICE IN THE LAMB)

Paka Felis atusc

For I will consider my Cat Jeoffry.

For in his morning orisons. he loves the Sun and the
Sun loves him. For he is of the tribe of Tiger.

For the Cherub Cat is a term of the Angel Tiger.

For he has the subtlety and hissing of a serpent, which in goodness
    he suppresses.

For he will not do destruction, if he is well-fed, neither will he spit
    without provocation.

For he purrs in thankfulness, when God tells him he's a good Cat.
    For he is an instrument for the children to learn benevolence
    upon.

For every house is incomplete without him and a blessing is
    lacking in the spirit.

For the Lord commanded Moses concerning the cats at the
    departure of the Children of Israel from Egypt.

For every family had one cat at least in the bag.

For the English Cats are the best in Europe.

For he is the cleanest in the use of his forepaws of any quadruped.
    For he is the quickest to his mark of any creature.

For he is tenacious of his point.

For he is a mixture of gravity and waggery.

For there is nothing sweeter than his peace when at rest. For there
    is nothing brisker than his life when in motion.

For he is of the Lord's poor and so indeed is he called by
    benevolence perpetually—

Poor Jeoffry! poor Jeoffry! The rat has bit thy throat.

For the divine spirit comes about his body to sustain it
in the complete cat.

CHRISTOPHER SMART (1722-1791)

For his tongue is exceeding pure so that it has in purity what it
    wants in music.
For he is docile and can learn certain things.
For he can set up with gravity which is patience upon approbation.
    For he can fetch and carry, which is patience in employment.

For he can jump over a stick which is patience upon proof positive.
    For he can spraggle upon waggle at the word of command.
For he can jump from an eminence into his master's bosom. For he
    can catch the cork and toss it again.
For he is hated by the hypocrite and miser.
For he camels his back to bear the first notion of business. For he
    made a great figure in Egypt for his signal services. For his ears
    are so acute that they sting again.
For from this proceeds the passing quickness of his attention.

For by stroking of him I have found out electricity.
For I perceived God's light about him both wax and fire.
For the Electrical fire is the spiritual substance, which God sends
    from heaven to sustain the bodies both of man and beast.
For, tho he cannot fly, he is an excellent clamberer.
For his motions upon the face of the earth are more than any
    other quadruped. For he can tread to all the measures upon the
    music.
For he can swim for life. For he can creep.

PELICAN

Philippe de Tawn
from a French Bestiary, 1160

Pelican[6] is the true name of a bird
Whose habitat is uniquely in Egypt.
Two kinds live close to the Nile I've heard
The same pelican painted in the crypt.

One dwells in water and lives on fish. Seek
Neighbor islands with the crocodile,
Lizard, serpent, stinking beasts. In Greek
He is onokrotalos. Not bad natured or vile.

In Latin they are *longum rostrum*, long face.
In French they are *lunc bec*. And when
Children come, they are beautiful with grace.
Kids fondle them, fingering a wing as with a pen.

The tiny birds love to play. Yet craving meat,
The parents torture them bleakly.
Dreadfully peck out their eyes. Slay them, eat,
And abandon them to death. But on the

Third day, they return. Lamenting the dead, see
How they peck their own bodies. Blood falls like strife
On the young birds who revive. Blood can be
Of quality, so the pelican comes to life.

---

6 It is often claimed that the Pelican poem from a French Bestiary, 1160, may
be oldest lyric poem in French, perhaps contemporary with the epic *La
Chanson de Roland*, (The Song of Roland).

In Kenya the favorite lake in which the pelican is found is Lake Nakuru. When
you walk near, suddenly thousands and thousands of pelicans fly into the
sky, blackening the sun. They are known to fly as 10,000 feet above the land.
(Ονοκρόταλος (Greek) – Onokrotolos-Pelican).

HOODED VULTURE

Tai iliyofunikwa
Necrosyrtes monachus

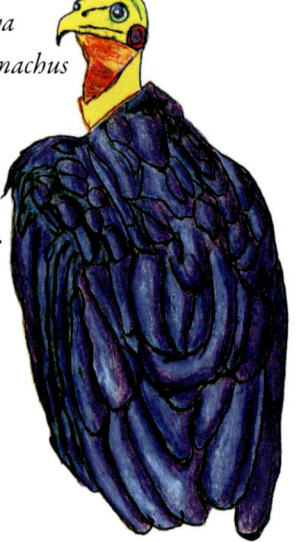

The hooded vulture is found in abundance
Until gamblers hear it brings them luck.
Sickies hear it heats the organs in their pants.
Vultures are threatened by every schmuck

Who thinks this garbage collector of dead
Animals must be poisoned so a medicine
From their flesh might spin their kids ahead
In school, expanding intellect. Gross sin

Of stupidity! Oddly, these vultures hang around
Universities. African students say
They defecate on them once a month. Such sound
With rubbish! Save the bird from traders, fools,

And grow the jungles so they can nest. Turns out
We are the horrid vultures. Our unfollowed rules
Anoint hunters and thieves with license. Vultures shout
Soundlessly for rescue from brutal us. Alas,

Even the name "vulture" is a curse. The bird's no worse
Or better than other beasts. They are first-class
Combatants for food. Permit them survival in our universe,
And some crazy day, since they are elegant

And in costume, let them swagger down Madison
Avenue In blue cloak as stunning as Jacob's coat
Of many colors. Come salvation! For now, we rue
Disappearance. Let them be common as a goat!

A NOBLE STINK IN PARADISE

My brother was not a camel driver,
a coward, shallow-hearted like a beast.
——Al-Khansa (575-646)

Triangle humped the camel is herd safe
      Like cows from tiger teeth.
He is not a savanna wandering waif
But a protected slave. No wreath
          Of blood
          On mud

For working camels. Horses cannot stand
      Their stink. In combat they
Disorient the cavalry. A band
Of dromedaries drives away
          Dragoons
          Of swoon-

ing armies, and in Ethiopia their milk's
      An aphrodisiac
For mystic sex strolling on Sun in silks
Of Paradise. Their Persian sack
          Of fat
          In hump hat

Dignity, reveals a solemn friend
      Whose coat like cashmere wool
Counters our chills, whose udders yield a blend
Of cheese and yoghurt bloating us full
          Like priests.
          These beasts

Of burden, milked on a small Kenyon far
    Whose coats lack the Sheik of Aral
Desert glamour. Old camels roast. Harm
less, lost-eyed, they wait to be
        Sweet meat
        To eat.

ORANGUTANG FILM STAR OF THE JUNGLE

Ngagi Gorilla beringei
(Eastern gorilla)

We are big time. One of our kings,
Kong, a royal mountain of an ape,
A learned lover who can spring
Sun high to glow and make us gape
    Stunned by a wisdom star
      Trapezing far

Above the jungle tent, from cloud
To cloud, to wow his lady, but
A serious lord. he leaves the loud
Grunting of tribal pals, and puts
    Knuckle ropes on the wind
      And agile mind

And heart in books from long ago.
He reads Hugo, sees his *Hunchback
of Notre Dame*, Quasimodo,
A prince of soul and passion, lack-
    ing a safe habitat
      Like a chased rat.

He must learn to lurch and love with no
Mad mob cramping his dream to be
A poet– singer and to solo
A gypsy emerald, and flee
    With her from the crude gang
      About to hang

His princess. They all die. Ugly
Hunchback and young gypsy. Depressed,
Kong turns to cinema. Soon he,
A show gorilla chained, oppressed,
    Breaks free, climbs the Empire
        State Building, fire

In his great arms, a blonde, *Beauty Kills*
Beast, they say. No way! Mighty yells
At circling aircraft. One lets fly
A shot. He tumbles into Hell....
    But the true Congo ape,
        Weeps & plans escape

From poachers who shoot him for bush
Meat, from woodcutters who chop his
Jungle for cities. His future is lewd—
Zoos or murder from King Kong's brood,
    But lives on dream and with
        A public myth.

GORILLA

Gorillas are the Fred Astaire of beings tap dancing on forest glades.
Some of these wonders slide on forest floors like the King of Spades.
"Gorilla" comes from ancient Greek Γόριλλαιm meaning "tribe
Of hairy women" as Carthaginian Hanno yelps in a diatribe.

The females prefer to ice skate on still frozen lakes or ponds
Or knuckle walk like famed judo specialists through bamboo grounds
Where Queen Victoria sets up her diamond table to play cards
With frustrated lovers who prefer gorillas to fussy, creaky bards.

Smart gorillas tall as ancient Greek bronzes like to nest
In trees. Deep sleep 12 hours without gulping Tylenol. Their best
Meals are leaves, ants, termites, fungi, and lots of shiny fruit.
They rarely drink water, but consume morning dew and loot

The hills for blueberry cake with birthday candles and jam
For summer dessert. Very brave when in a jam, they ham
It up, risk lives for wife and terrain. When chimps try to steal,
The maestro gorilla grabs a branch, wields it like a steel

Club, and every animal flees the raging ancestor of us all
(Though a few genes off). Like a friend at a Fireman's Ball,
When a gorilla is your pal, you leap like a mirrored kite
Above the galaxies and jitterbug through a croning clarinet night.

DWARF MONGOOSE

A mongoose means terror for a snake,
But our dwarf painting fits into a shoebox. So, don't shake
Unless you're a frog or spider. It has a pal,
The yellow hornbill. They discuss Blaise Pascal
And his theory of being, boasting they
Don't have to prove they exist in Bombay

Or on a page. Eat, survive, have a family,
And stroll safely is their dream book. We
Chase the same vision. The lady mongoose
Leads these nomads. Let them loose
And they eat meat, a termite or egg,
And if bored, they hit Russia, a powder keg

Of experts, and clothe them in tuxedos,
A dignified stance. Sew them in prose
Of Hemingway's Moveable Feast.
Our dwarf is a giant beauty, the priest
Of cutability. Don't fear. It is wise,
Dwelling in dream like eternal sunrise.

KUDO

Tandala Mkubwa/Tandala Ndogo
Tragelaphus strepsiceros

The creature of the stainless corkscrew horn
Twisting twice and a half—enough to lock
Horns with a rival male in spring—feels horn-
    y and creates a brash newborn.

Strange beauty—true beauty is aberration—
This acrobat of joy floats on the wind,
And at top speed he hasn't left the station
    Or so it seems. In his elation,

The antelope looks like a rocking horse
Bounding up from its base. Bopping to heaven,
He's Sancho Panza on his cosmic course
    And the same mad dreamer hoarse,

Vocalizing love screams, he to his kudu
Lady. Bravo. He's human just like us.
Morality tale. He likes his ways to You!
    Even if he must take a bus!

ANIMAL FIESTA

We Africans came first. Surely, we began
In hydrothermal vents below the sea
Where carbon molecules in a pulsing
Chemosynthesis made organic soup.
After four billon years some tetrapods
Dump fish-life for the shore. They eat and poop
And evolve into creatures. Soon lions stroll
And wise antelopes saunter round the globe,
Breeding and spreading genes. Our honor roll
Is roam, survive, be painted on a cave wall
And play on prairies. We know *la belle vie*.
Josephine Baker whips up our animal ball,
Leopards and chimps hoop in a thorn tree,
& our bat king whistles like a nightingale.

IMPALA

Swala

Epyceros Melampus

The impala prances in his red-flame boots
Across the meadow. Catch me if you can!
Felines are the enemy. So long toots.
Off he dives like the quarter Moon. A fan
Of fever trees bows dust in killer's eyes.
In his green trousers and a glossy coat, he bounds
On bushland, perfect for a browser. Wise
To predators, if caught, the battlegrounds
Will stink with purple blood. In bluish horn,
He races like his son, Chevrolet
Impala, and beats lightning. Not forlorn
He celebrates free days, chanting a lay
He picked up from a gurgling pond. He'll jump
Over a cloud to Sun, mumbling no grump.

WATERBUCK OBSERVED

Tundu la maji
Kobus ellipsiprymnus

One life is long and hope is infinite
    Stars dashing through no-time dark.
A black and white buck sits forever on a plain
    Soon to wriggle as real estate
For entrepreneurs whose love is bucks,
    Too, a green dollar's eye.

So no more antelopes seated by water holes.
    They sit staring at you
In city zoos. Bad future. Who can dazzle
    And persuade to save the beast?
I can't. Read this and see roaming beasts
    Tap dancing in Africa where

Only millennia ago all of us tread away
    From Sun to green pastures
Isaiah promised for the saved in new
    Continents. Nothing as rich
With magnificence as Bible animals
    Adam discovers in dream.

The buck sits contemplating tricky
    Trigonometry. He sees Plato's
Assertion that mathematics is the brain
    Of the universe and counts
The sand and Earth and trees and flights
    Of cliff eagles. Smart antelope.

When he stops, he leaves his imprint on
   The Moon, kibitzing blue
With pleasure. At this conjunction of Greek
   Genius and animal vision,

The visionary beast rises and climbs. He climbs
   Sunrays & glows as our true Sun.

GEMBOK

Tai iliyofunikwa
Necrosyrtes monachus

The gemsbok or South African oryx
Is big. Namibia blares it on its coat
Of arms. Its black streaks gleam like onyx,
Though below its nose beams a white note.
Alas, their splendid horns bring them death
From horrid hunters. They like the desert,
Survive on scant water. And hold your breath!
Favored foods are melons and cucumber.

They are also polygamous, meaning a lot
Of girlfriends to mate with. So, a female
Gemsbok chases a handsome gent. A bigshot.
New Mexico bought some. There they sail
Gallantly, not attacked by leopard or lion,
And our American cougar is too small
To murder it. We must adore this Zion
Of grace. It could clearly win any masked ball.

GOODNIGHT, SWAN

Goodnight, evening swan.
See you floating in the dawn.

Farewell, lover in tower.
See you in your morning shower.

Farewell, evening bliss.
Catch you in a daybreak kiss.

Goodnight, midnight love.
Hear you laughing like a dove.

So long, bright gazelle,
Tap, tap your mystic bell.

Cheerio, buffalo,
Plod slow, **PICASSO**.

Catch you soon,
Bouncing baboon.

Au revoir elephant,
Floating in the firmament.

Goodnight, evening star,
Meet you at a lunar bar.

Good morning, bumble bee
Spot you in an apple tree.

Bye-bye, butterfly
Hear you in a lullaby.

AFRICAN HONEYBEE

Bees are an annoying pest who makes honey and wax
And cleverly toot a golden sax.
Their delightful honey helps a cough
And you feel more decadent than a Romanoff.
In sub-Sahara Africa no fret. There is no bear
To crash into your hive and steal your underwear.
From honey wax, you make candles and soap
To light a room or clean your telescope.
But beware of bee warfare. Too many a sting
Might kill a clown or **BAUDELAIRE** in Beijing.
Like bats, bees pollinate flowers and so
A bee helps flower-stores make a mound of dough.
The queen bee bosses the tremble-dancing worker.
They all survive fine in Africa's hot temperature.
Beware! Bees in Africa remain colonialists. Each colony
Is austerely proud and bites when you steal honey.

BEASTS

Something inspires the only cow of late
To make no more of a wall than an open gate.
—Robert Frost (1874-1963)

This book of beasts shows the wild animal
    Roaming on a playground
And battleground of combat where the male
    Knocks male for mating ground,
Where carnivore and herbivore stand locked
    In standoff, deadly fights
Raging for blood like human wars to mock
    All beauty day and night

In high savanna and bush. They keep alive
    The eco balance of
Jungle and plain where the will to survive,
    Not sentimental love,
Commands. Yet with hope against hope, fierce grace
    Grows like the tons of weed
To keep a hippo fed. A leopard's face,
    A gazelle's leap are seed

Of Earthly mystery, and the warted brow
    Of the warthog is wonder
For a Punch and Judy show. And then the cow.
    Domestically for plunder,
From her four teats hundreds of pounds of milk
    Can feed an army wild
With thirst, whose victory is sweet liquid silk
    From nature's holy child.

SACRED COW

The cow is sacred for Samburu and Maasai,
    Not as in India where
She's roaming god. For pastoralists she's sky
    And Earth, and be aware
She is the food, the dowry, and comrade
    Of the warrior with
His spear for hunt, his knife for turning bad
    Invaders into myth,

And for his wife or wives who circumcised,
    Alas, work just as hard
Building the temporary huts comprised
    Of dung and mud, and guard
Them just as fiercely when a panga gang
    Or Idi Amin's thugs
Shoot up the huts for cattle. Women hang
    And crush the captured bugs

And know no fear. Stoic like sacred beasts
    Samburu feed on blood
And fat they cut from cattle for their
    Feasts, or meat, the finest grub
For supper when they splurge and eat a chunk
    Of bovine flesh. At night
They dance and chant, slamming their long spear
    On Earth when they take flight

And join the sky. On weekends they go
    Up to mountains for
A chat with gods. Their cows live in the eye

Of rain clouds who restore
The arid bush, which isn't Paradise
　　Or Hell, but what for now
Is true. How long? Progress is fatal lice.
　　Long live their sacred cow!

The wild beasts will survive because of parks
　　But naked tribes with heart
Fare deadly when the grimy city barks
　　To clothe them and their art.
I cannot bear that day that's almost come,
　　Yet cheerfully I keep
My eye on what has been and is. Now mum,
　　Tomorrow we can weep.

LAUGHING DOVE

The dove is peace. Slam her as raven, crow,
Pigeon or any tribal slur, the dove
Is peace. She is dream, and dreamers know,
And Blake and Shakespeare sing: enduring love
Is best, not swordplay in the street, nor curse.
Hear somewhere a dove. William Blake may bow
To chimney sweepers. He pities the whore's hearse,
Loves black and white. Please hear. Blake's living now,

His heart bigger than Quijote's fantastic nag.
Noah sends out a peace dove over the flood
To see where land begins. Hope is her tag.
Let us not kill again. Do not spill blood
The dove keeps singing, "Do not sacrifice
A single soul." Consider your own luck.
John of the Cross implores a dove's advise
And flies high like a dove, drops into muck

To find mystical love where night is white
And finds her in the dark night of the soul.
A laughing dove eats fruit and seeds to fight
Off hunger. Saints and doves cry from a hole.
Will peace calm plains of lion and the lamb?
Will murder cease on Kenya's wild savanna?
Will poacher dine with ranger, build a wise dam,
Dig waterholes from Gabon to Botswana?

HUMAN COMPOSERS OF MANY ANIMALS

**WILLIAM SHAKESPEARE
AND HIS HELLHOUNDS**

**MIGUEL DE CERVANTES' DON QUIJOTE
AND HIS WONDER HORSE ROCINANTE**

**JUAN DE LA CRUZ IN
HIS DARK NIGHT OF FLAME**

JUAN ANTONIO DE LA PEÑA, VOLUNTEER ARRAGONESE PARK WARDEN

Park volunteer Juan Antonio likes to roast fish over coals,
But he won't touch a rib of meat. Tall as a cloud. he rolls
Around the meadows like a wise giraffe. He's no slouch

Or amateur. Like Goya, Aragon's Juan Antonio will crouch
For hours to watch, paint, guard an oryx or roaming heron
Who reminds him of Argentine Basques who in barren

Wilderness in Patagonia horseback with glee,
Exuding South Pole majesty of elephant seal and scholarly
Examiners of climate, star-high gales, and melting ice

So, our globe might have a future better than cooked rice
Nourishing and perishing in Chinese bellies with
Historic pride. No Cultural Revolution or myth

Of extremism in Juan. Juan Antonio is a good, smart guy,
A bloke with a beautiful mission of focusing his magnifying eye
On poacher, enemy of beast, and mean trafficker

Of piano ivory and rhino skull, who turn a beast to blur
Of stolen being. Good Juan. Why must a sweetheart
Disappear for greed? He also has life plans. He will chart

The sumptuous mountains of the rugged Basque
Countryside when he returns to Spain. His sole task
Now is animal guardian. Then, a crime bullet bangs

Into his forehead. Apparitions gone. Juan Antonio's future hangs.
Park volunteer Juan Antonio likes to roast fish over coals,
But he won't touch a rib of meat. Tall as a cloud he strolls.

JUAN ANTONIO DE PEÑA

ANIMALS ARE ETERNAL LIKE
THE LILAC-BREASTED ROLLER

Roller ya matiti ya lilac
Coracias caudatus

Animal, mineral, stone. The animal
Must and will survive. They are able
To live a thousand years—
These figures on the bush. Their mystery
Is clean. They race with blue majesty,
Believe their arts. No silly fears!

Animals are also gods. All can see
The human divinity of four-legs
And monkeys too. A moving rapture.
There's some chance to wake not to cracked eggs
But barrels of wine and cognac. Adventure
In the wild must be by eyes, not murder lead.

When hope is banished, beasts drop dead.
Animal, mineral, stone. The animal
Must and will survive. They are able
To live a thousand years—
These figures on the bush. Their mystery
Is clean. They race with blue majesty.

GOLDEN PANTHER BAKES
BREAD FOR HALLOWEEN

Ring all the bells! The golden panther who excels in baking bread
Has dropped down from Jupiter to raise the sullen dead

Who are cursing in their graves for indifferent Sun
To shake them back to fleshly love or swallowing a hot cross bun.

Then, penguin ghosts in the South Pole tango all the way
Back to Good Gales Buenos Aires where they curse or pray

For saints bones or Spanish cheese to make angels cart
Them across the ice into lollypop joy of a nasty fart,

Even a nasty belch might do, anything to make life shocking real
On All Hallows Day. In Spain they place pastries on graves to steal

Souls back into life, setting bones on graveyard, and light
Bonfires to welcome the dead on their return. They drink to fight

Evil spirits. People drift from house to house, reciting verse
For food, their faces painted black. Leave food for ghosts. Could
  be worse

That on this unholy day, beggars celebrate free food and drink
Not only for the dead but hungry living souls who in humble bodies
  stink.

Early as the 16th century, people go in costume from house to house,
Collecting gifts left for them, from bread down to a tiny louse.

While people wander, Church bells ring to frighten witches,
The Brits observe 5 November as a celebration against sons of-bitches

Catholics who plan to kill the Protestant King James 1 and his
    Parliament.
So it's known as Gunpowder Treason Day. And Puritans don't lament

The bonfires of hated "traitors." So, 18th century children are in a
    begging mood
For money on effigies of Guy Fawkes. But Later In Catholic Italy they
    leave abundant food

For hungry souls who dance invisibly over grateful graves.
Souls are represented by a BJack-O-Lantern who saves

The spirts and fights the Devil. Lots of drink on Halloween
On which wondrous spirits fill their hopes with the unseen!

Even the Golden Panther gets drunk for good harvests and joy.
Children trick or treat in masks. Lovely time. The panther likes its
    wondrous rollercoaster toy.

BLACK PANTHER

Mweusi
Black Panther

The panther is handsomest of quadrupeds.
He is black and a map of white dots threads
Around his body. Having fed on ample prey,
He harbors in a cave and sleeps. On the next day

He rises from the Earth and truly roars.
From his deep throat a sweet aroma pours
That is richer than exhilarating balm.
The animals who hear his voice soon are calm.

They follow him, dazed in tender ecstasy.
All follow him. Only red serpents flee
The panther, or they weaken when they hear

His howl and hide in caves, dreading to appear.
The panther is the handsomest quadruped
His pearl-dotted body is black like Russian bread.

GREEN HORSE FOR A CHILD IN NAMIBIA

In Egypt horses thrive when Alexander the Great created
Alexandria, and camel, horse and elephant get the bid

To linger on the landscape. In war, horses are bold,
Daringly save lives. Today they are racehorse gold

And in poorest gold-desert lands like Namibia,
A girl dreams of a Horse of Gold from far Abyssinia

Or Cairo. If not a real horse, then, a red or blue horse
Printed on a canvas wall. Scream until hoarse,

Still no gift for the young girl. What to do? Go back
Again to Greece, and behold in your knapsack

A splendid gift. Not to ride on but to glare
At. Her bronze **HORSE OF GREEN**. The child asks you to share.

WILD DONKEY

Panda Pori
Equus Africanus

The leg of this wild ass resembles a zebra leg.
3 million years ago, in Idaho, where a powder keg

Erupts and sends the donkey/zebra everywhere,
Confusing then with domestic horse and so tear

Differences apart. After that 19th century ass skull,
The academy argues who is who. A lot of bull

Turning these beauties in Ethiopia and Somalia
Into endangered species like koalas in Australia.

The donkey does its part, outracing cheetah and lion,
Preparing for Olympic trials. Even a dandelion

Hides from murderers by posing as a fallen moon.
Crooks who try to kill them hear the donkey scream like a typhoon

About to drown these Ethiopic hunters for a fake medical miracle.
The African wild ass is not on a Ship of Fools, but a lyrical

Creature nature issues from its laws. The Jewish Bible extols
Them as indigenous royalty. In Sumeria the donkey tolls,

Pulls wagons in the 3rd millennium. Now, they endure 3 days
Without drinking water. But the present phase

For this super animal is grim. Some 600 in the world,
Yes, mainly in zoos. Save them from plodding only the underworld!

YELLOW BUTTERFLY ON THE ROAD

On great horizons in Africa, you're not a bore.
        Over an impala you soar
And silent as the roaring Sun from far,
        You map the atlas of our Star.
You beautify the lands. The rich and poor
        In eye and soul see you explore.
From Casa Blanca to Stonetown City in Zanzibar,
        You brighten every black harbor.

YELLOW HORNBILL

Hornbill ya Njano
Tockus leucomelas

These beauty birds with their yellow gold beak
Recall golden elevators in the Woolworth Building in New York,
Yet their eyeballs illuminate the Heavens with a streak
Of impossibility. Their bill is a gold-plated fork
Helmeted and filled with ivory, a battering ram
For aerial jousts. Hornbills reflect a forest in a jam.
They're also monogamous. No horsing around
With other chicks. As to rivals, they butt them to the ground.
Like other birds their vision is binocular, but to their aid
Huge eyelashes umbrella their eyeballs into shade.
Hornbills love to follow monkeys spitting up insects in a cascade
Of delicious breakfast, luncheon, and supper. Like every animal
In Africa, they live in danger as savannas shrink. But not all
Is bad for hornbills. No bullet slams them in the sky & Africa
Accords them Great Kili as her breezy dancehall.

WATTLED CRANE

Orongo ndevu
Grus carunculata

This crane is like a long-legged heron,
Stands in fields like Moon reflecting a steel hand-iron;
He discerns small rodents and far fish as soul flesh
He can devour and consume fresh.

His solid stare is critical
As for every animal,
Warning of danger as well as chance
To win desserts so he might prance

Full-bellied for another day and night.
This beauty gobbles meat. His sight
Could put an optometrist in the street,
For his eyes are a telescope, his gaze discreet

Until he nabs a victim. Cruelty and pain do not concern
This beauty (to our eyes). He jabs his beak to earn
His lunch. We must not be critical of the animal
Who kills to live another day and steady his moral.

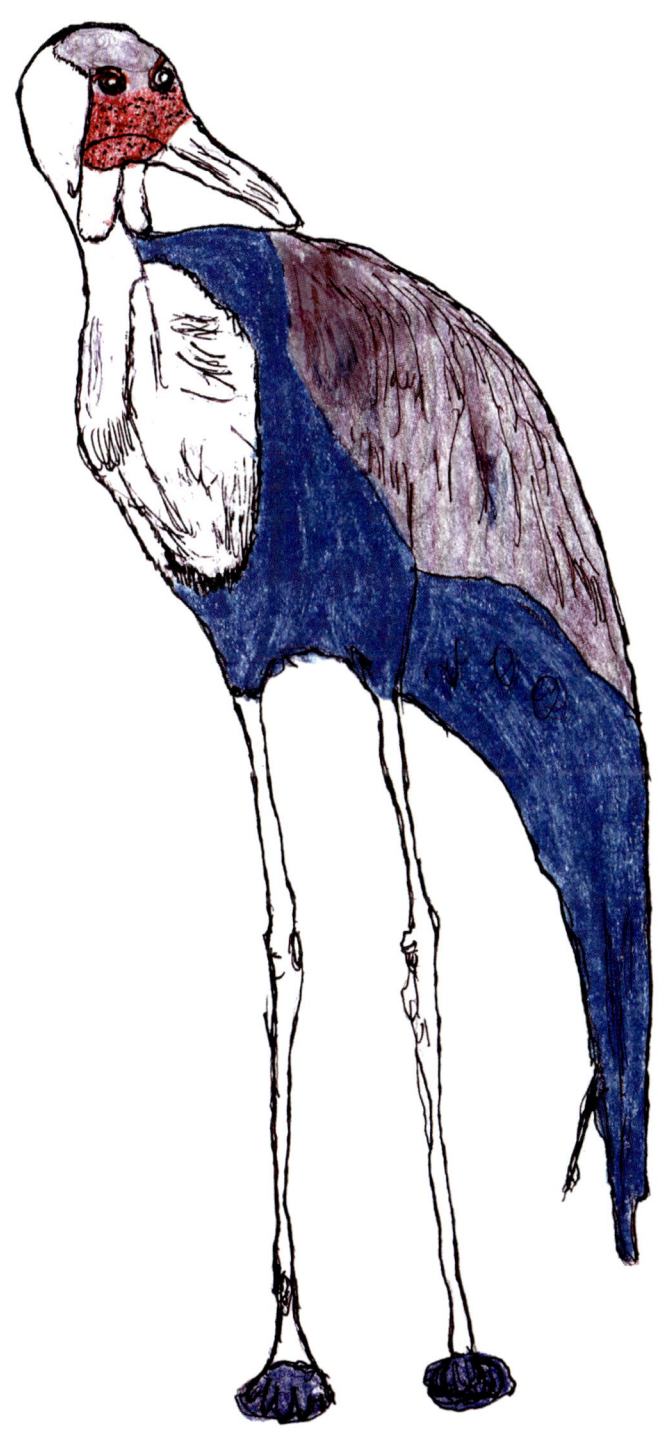

SERVAL, NEPHEW OF THE PARD & MIGHTY TIGER

Mtumwa

Leptailurus serval

The nimble serval is a feline first class.
When racing, black lightning issues from his rear brass!

It easily leaps 7 feet to nail a bird,
With longest cat legs for its size. It sneaks unheard,

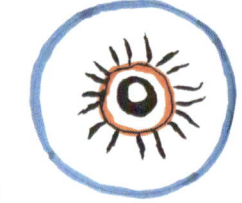

Then bolts from Earth to bite its prey. It's beautiful,
As leopards are, but beauty here means a mouth full

Of meat. Diverse diet—rat, bird, insect, reptile—
With a bite on neck or head. This spotted cat has style,

Looks like an overseas cousin, the Nahuatl ocelot,
Whom he resembles in shape and spot.

Like all African beasts we hope he will survive
Modernity, greed, and gangsters who make animals nosedive.

For now, this dancer on the meadow charms,
But best not to cradle him in your arms!

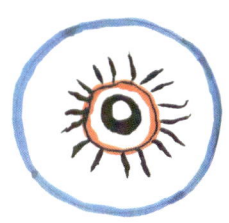

CRAFTY ARDWOLF

Fisi mdogo
Proteles cristata

The aardwolf is nocturnal in his feast,
Eating carnal remnants of some gloomy beast

Not swift enough to dodge the cheetah's daytime jaws.
By night the aardwolf bloodies his robust paws

So he can dance and prance along the plain
Until he finds enough goodies to flood his brain

With thrill. He's cool and strong, a hyena of the night.
When daylight comes, he hides from feline sight

Yet dreams of joining a roving opera. There, clad in blue
He'd woo a crowd and solicit meat to keep his focus true.

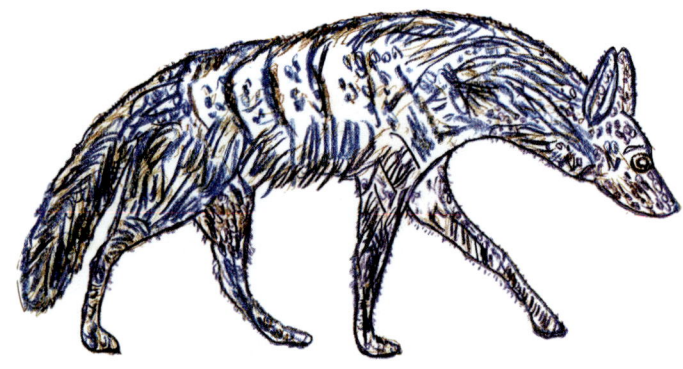

NOCTURNAL CIVET

Mzing

Nandinia binotat

The civet is a beautiful and introverted fellow
Who sleeps amid dense African vegetation.
When Sun dives into safe mellow
Gloom, the civet assumes its station,
Hunting reptiles, berries, and leaps for fruit.
So, with rapacious eye, dolled in a checkered suit,
It bites and gulps good supper. Finest treat
Is hamburger of snake and bushmeat
Of rat, mice, and egg. The civet is no slouch.
With zealous teeth it seeks grub to jam into its pouch
For savanna pudding. Beware!
The civet is turning rare.
Prairie thugs kill the amazing cat! Its prized civetone
Incites slaughter. With it, perfumers build their bloodstone.

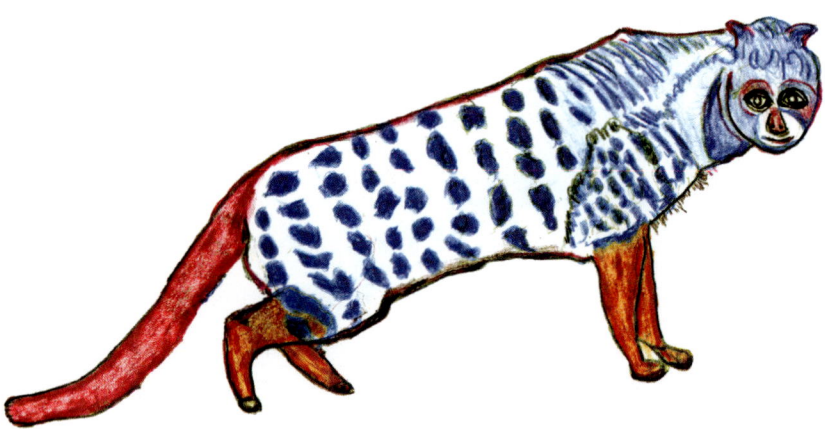

KLIPSPRINGER STAR

Mbuzi mawe
Oreotragus oreotragus

When chetah Sun, leopard Moon and klipspringer star
Drink beer at a celestial bar,
Constellations giggle, North Star sweats,
And Pegasus gallops and wets

Our globe with champagne, coke, and speckled tea
Unique to Zanzibar's concealed songsters on a spree.
Caruso and Victoria de los Ángeles croon to Heaven
And collude to turn Monte Carlo into leaven

To bake Virgin Stars for dames who sleep
Solely with prince or king! Deep
In gravity, Einstein with computer
And Saint Exupéry in bullet-proof Le Maine fur

Show hope for Girard Manley Hopkins scrawling in sprung
Rhythm his Terrible Sonnets holding honey, dung,
Hope & beauty! Splendid Hopkins. Solely, Anthony
Hopkins might orate Girard's poems about Marcus Antony

& Cleopatra, whose deaths upon Caesar Augustus's sword don't deter
That magic couple from being Queen and Master
Of our rollicking Earth. Hooray for Rome's cosmos.
Every splendid blue-black Moon and ghost morose

Or bellicose is eager to paint the splashing sky
With Willy Shakespeare's melancholy cherry pie.
With crimson pancakes, songing whales, and a chubby hunk of Billy
Cheetah sun, leopard Moon, & klipspringer star, never silly,

You cultivate soul and astronomer joying bazaars! You may drip blood,
Klipspringer, but your name proves you a champion
Alive despite feline jaws. If caught, you battle on
With fury legs and horns. Even the fabled lion may be mud.

SABLE ANTELOPE

Swala sable

Big sable antelopes like to chew bones
For minerals; grass and weeds and lyric tones.

When fighting other bulls, they strike from their knees;
When lions attack, beware, those big cats ease

Into feline eternity. Newborns have sandy coats
So they can camouflage as in Zanzibar boats

Tied like wild kites to wave-bolted docks
To wrestle the Indian Ocean and her flocks

Of guinea hens flecked with diamonds and salt,
And so, the sable antelope drinks stars to exalt

His posture on the savanna. O, O, O! What fun
To race against this great deer! You've won

By chewing seaweed and ketchup, enough
To unhinge ravenous foes. You're shining tough

With enemies. Otherwise, you spend your evening
Studying math and Percy Bysshe Shelley for deep sing.

Wish you eternity and 4 weeks of safety & pleasures.
Heaven has an attic for your astral endeavors

And Earth keeps you alive in South Africa where
For 22 years you hit the road, strolling on air.

BLUE ANTELOPE, AN IMAGINARY ANIMAL

I am a splendid imaginary animal.
Compared to prison zoos, our Kenya bush is a ball.

I dodge the hunters' bullets from ground and plane.
Save me from extermination, or you, world, are insane!

There's no one blue like me bouncing like a Chaplin clown
Until lead hits my brain. Then, I too shut down.

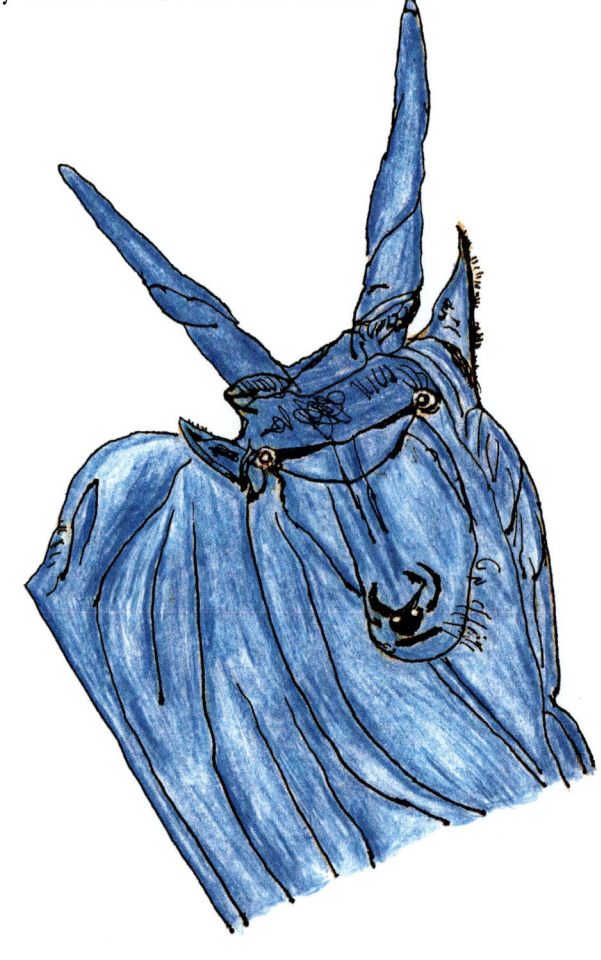

BONGO

Ubongo
Tragelaphus eurycerus

The bongo, once Prince of the Congo, big guy with great looks
Which makes him a unique hunter victim.
So, there exist less than 100 in parks.
Greed kills them. They nose-dive to a poacher's whim.

The bongo is a nocturnal chap
Trotting through woods. Few humans see them pose
With their twisting horns, their precious skullcap,
They race through tangles of lianas, close

To Earth. & with long tongues they grab leaves
And grass for eats. They are saved for a while
When legend claims that if obnoxious thieves
Murder them, the bums will have epilepsy

And croak. Now it's free shots. As ghostly beast,
They hide in night. In dark their beauty wins
The dimmest heart, but even a high priest
Can't lessen slaughter. Guns have evil fins.

AUSTERE PURPLE GRENADIER

Kitendeli Tumbo-zambarau
Uraeginthus ianthinogaster

The purple grenadier is not a true grenade launcher
Against savannah enemies. Its best weapon is its voice
With which it calls lovers, and not to conquer
Bush enemies. When heard, like a sailor's choice,

It flies to the ecstatic spot, and nature's impulse
Commands. Then back to its feathered nest.
It fares fine on African meadows and isn't cold.
It can't bare the cold. Its song is amazingly bold

And embodies its fame as a beauty that makes
It a favorite Western pet. Ouch! I hear it scream!
We call its Western cousins "canaries"

And pamper them like trimming an apple tree.
Our colorful soprano beauty muses on the West with rage.
Why? Don't be an ass, reader! In Africa, this purple canary is free,
Not locked up for petting in a cage!

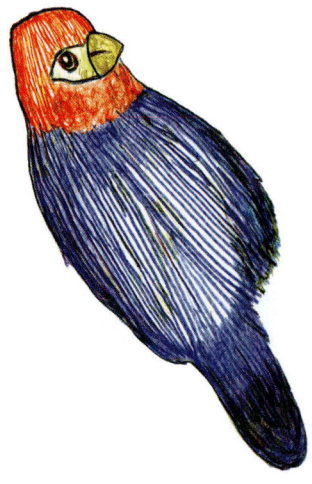

AFRICAN CROWNED CRANE

Gibbericeps

You big beauties are dancers when you breed,
Tango pros, who gladly slip into waltz.
You are extravagant, but never schmalz
And don't wait for vacations to seed

New cranes and create a colorful tribe.
You are majesty, an insect-wolfing duke
Or princess. Off in a marsh, you bribe
Heavens for rain and love to spook

A bloated spider with your deadly beak.
So long, tiny octopean monster.
You master of grace will soon break
Its fly-obsessed mouth. You'll stir

It in your golden cheeks. Body alone
Is not your Pike's Peak. You meditate
Smoother than Buddhists and intone
Your thought, chant, and illuminate.

MARABOU STORK

Marabou
Leptoptilos crumenifer

Some say it is the undertaker bird
Because of its behind's shape. That's absurd
As it's foul. Birders say its name means hermit,
Untrue & strange. This huge bird can hardly fit
Anywhere but in the free sky. And there
It dives, connives, does air tricks to make its bare
Huge head ready to plunge at any food,
Living or skeletal. Doesn't like a human dude,
Luckily. It has a naked head, easy to keep clean
When its feathered scalp's inside a victim. They lean
On anything left over by vultures including a shoe,
Might be called "donkey of the heavens." Marabou
Feathers often adorn hats. Alas, the bird's huge,
Easy to spot and shoot. Easy victim of any scrooge.

KORI BUSTARD

Ardeotis kori struthiunculus

The heaviest flying mammal, our astronaut bird,
With 9-foot wingspan needs space. Won't be deterred
By other soaring beasts. Won't hang out in a green wood,
Yet likes to trot around looking for a beetle or tasty lizard, or good

Small snakes it gobbles like mellow waffles. Bustards eat seed, and
   lock
Their eyes on berries and melons. They are called "gum peacock"
Because they love Acacia gum. In mating, the male
Is flamboyant Romeo. The ladies inspect him from beak to tail

Until he spreads his wings. Then, the female barks, and soon
Come glossy eggs she hides from ostriches or any goon
Who'll rob her nest. To keep clean, Kori will bathe in sun and dust
And stand for hours in shade, and mistrust.

A kibitzing fowl who likes to schmooze,
Then, slurp and hop off with a beak filled with booze.
Many enemies surround—leopard, cheetah, lion—
Even baboons hop in. Worst is the would-be Zion

Of the plain, when calm as a dandelion, the leopard feline
Appears in its flamboyant blue jean,
Bites and wolfs the bustard down. Kori persists in chalk on cave walls,
And on the Bush. Hear it from the North Star. Magic calls.

SCIMITAR KNIFE ORYX

Scimitar Mume
Oryx Dammah

This huge buck, almost extinguished by wicked hunter,
Is graceful in gate as a professional punter.
In ancient Egypt they are domesticated and food
Of gods, yet over-barbecued.

For endurance, this buck trots waterless.
In extreme heat, it sleeps. Tragically, the oryx is a mess
Of torn meat when hunters get the buzz.
Left intact is a white-and-brown fuzz.

Ominously, the oryx almost goes extinct.
Miracle! Western conservationists link
Together 11,000 in Texas to 4,000 in Arab Gulf States
To bring the oryx back to Africa, male and mates.

It survives and thrives in protected sites
From Morocco to Qatar and her super-heat bites.
Magic! Today these thrifty-water bucks persist.
They have gloriously kissed

The hills and moors of Ethiopia's National Park
And can fill the Yankees baseball park.
The scimitar knife oryx is a reverberating joyful banjo.
Where they show, mountains and polar stars echo: GO!

GOLD BROWN RAM IN A SEASON OF PEACE

To everything there is a season,
A time to be born and a time to die,
A time to plant and a time to pluck up what is planted,
A time to kill and a time to heal,
A time to break down and a time to build up,
A time to weep and a time to laugh,
A time to mourn and a time to dance,
A time to cast stones and a time to gather them.
A time to embrace and a time to stop embracing.
A time to seek and a time to lose,
A time to keep and a time to throw away,
A time to tear and a time to sew,
A time to keep silent and a time to speak,
A time to love and a time to hate,
A time of war and a time for peace.

BLUE WILD RAM THROUGH CENTURIES

A Psalm for now. The Maasai and
Companion bovine have scant fear
Of dark. Their milk is sweet, not canned,
Air more delicious than a tear.

In Eden sings an Orphic bell,
Time comes and is our vital food on Earth.
Delight, forget all tolling bell.
Each breath of beast is a fresh birth.

Ram, will you bounce on a rocky path
When shivering skyscrapers fall
And people drown in bloodbath?
Will you hop at a sad masked ball?

You still ramble the wilderness bush
But your end is a slaughterhouse.
Your wandering is no goofy gold rush.
William Blake mourns you in a painting brush.

PARADISE

After six days the Earth is done.
And mythic animals know peace.
The lion and the ram have fun
And Milton films our Paradise
And grieves for every creature fled
Because we got too smart to be
Obedient and caged. So, we are fed
To time and an eternity

Of birth and dark and combat for Each
unknown day beyond the Wall:
Adventure, breath, and mind. We soar
Or gloom a while and then the fall
And we are past, but love's not gone. The
Beast has not our fear or hope.
It fully lives each comic dawn until
The night. Milton says nope:

A Paradise Regained exists,
Though Milton sonorous in style
Knows that no animal persists,
His *river-horse and scaly crocodile*
Are made to breathe and bungle through
Eternal now. Each animal,
Whether in combat zone or zoo,
Is a philosopher and never bawls.

A HEART IN WINTER

So, a heart in winter says, *No.*
There is time. Animals will thrive.
Who knows how, where? We cannot know,
But cannot yield to a swan dive
As we ignore the melting North Pole.
Let us help our keen ancestors,
The beasts from whom we came. Not drool
In loss. Thirst and beauty open doors.

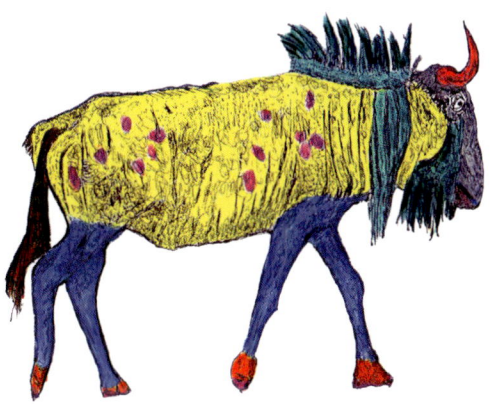

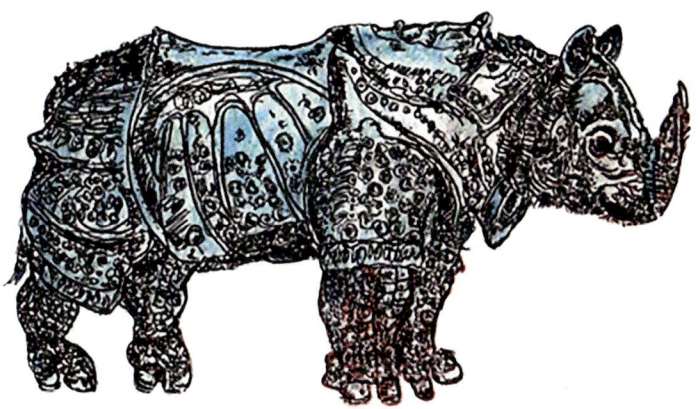

Alphabetical Index of Titles & Paintings

Gembok
Genet Cat
Giraffe, Grand Philosopher of Africa
Golden Brown Ram in a Season of Peace
Goodnight, Swan
Gorilla
Gray Crowned Crane
Green Horse
Guinea Fowl
Halcyon or Kingfisher
Heron
Hippopotamus
Hyena
Impala
Jackal
Jeoffry the Cat 1
Jeoffry the Cat 2
Juan Antonio de la Peña
Klipsinger
Kori Bustard
Kudo
Leopard Dancer
Lilac-Breasted Roller
Lion Sleeps with One Eye Open
Marabou Stork
Mosquito
Mythical Blue African Animal
Orangutang
Oryx
Owl
Owl (Alexander the Great)
Owl (Egyptian)
Painted Dog

Paradise
Parrot
Peacock
Ram in a Season of Peace
Red Butterfly
Red Ram
Rhinoceros
Sable Antelope
Sacred Cow
Salvation Sammy
Scimitar Knife Oryx
Serval
Spider
Swan
Sun
Termite
Tiger
Tiger (Rousseau)
Tortoise
Unicorn & Princess
Vervet Monkey
Waterbuck
Warthog
Wattled Crane
Whale
Wild Donkey
White Unicorn
William Blake
William Shakespeare
Unicorn & Princess
Yellow Hornbill
Zebra

BOOKS BY WILLIS BARNSTONE

Sweetbitter Love: Poems of Sappho, A New Translation. With Epilogue and Metrical Guide by William McCulloh.

The Poems of Mao Zedong.

The Complete Poems of Sappho.

Ancient Greek Lyrics.

Love Poems by Pedro Salinas: My Voice Because of You and Letter Poems to Katherine.

MEMOIR
With Borges on an Ordinary Evening in Buenos Aires: A Memoir.

Sunday Morning in Fascist Spain: A European Memoir (1948–1953).

We Jews and Blacks: Memoir with Poems: With a Dialogue and Poems by Yusef Komunyakaa.

LITERARY CRITICISM
The Poetics of Ecstasy: from Sappho to Borges.

The Poetics of Translation: History, Theory, Practice.

Borges at 80: Conversations & Photographs.

BIBLICAL & GNOSTIC
The Poems of Jesus Christ.

The Other Bible: Jewish Pseudepigrapha, Christian Apocrypha, Gnostic Scriptures, Kabbalah, Dead Sea Scrolls.

The Apocalypse: Book of Revelation.

The Art of Worldly Wisdom, by Gracian Baltazar. Co-translated by J. Joseph Jacobs.

The New Covenant: The Four Gospels and Apocalypse.

The Gnostic Bible: Gnostic Texts of Mystical Wisdom from the Ancient and Medieval Worlds—Pagan, Jewish, Christian, Mandaean, Islamic, and Cathar. Co-edited with Marvin Meyer.

The Restored New Testament Including The Gnostic Gospels of Thomas, Mary, and Judas.

ANTHOLOGIES / EDITIONS
Rinconete y Cortadillo by Miguel de Cervantes. Co-edited with Hugh A. Harter

Modern European Poetry. With co-editors Kimon Friar, Patricia Terry, Arthur Wensinger, George Reavy, Sonia Raiziss, Alfred de Palchi, and Angel Flores

Concrete Poetry: A World View, Co-edited with Mary Ellen Solt.

Eighteen Texts: Writings by Contemporary Greek Authors.

The Literatures of Asia, Africa, and Latin America, Co-edited with Tony Barnstone.

Literatures of Latin America.

Literatures of the Middle East, Co-edited with Tony Barnstone.

BLACK WIDOW PRESS MODERN POETRY SERIES

President of Desolation & Other Poems by Jerome Rothenberg

Barbaric Vast & Wild: An Assemblage of Outside & Subterranean Poetry from Origins to Present. Edited by Jerome Rothenberg and John Bloomberg-Rissman

Concealments and Caprichos by Jerome Rothenberg

Eye of Witness: A Jerome Rothenberg Reader. Edited by Heriberto Yepez and the author

Osiris with a trombone across the seam of insubstance by Julian Semilian

Soraya by Anis Shivani

Fractal Song by Jerry W. Ward, Jr.

Mikhail Yeryomin: Sixty Years, Selected Poems: 1957-2017 by Mikhail Yeryomin. Translated and edited by J. Kates

BLACK WIDOW PRESS POETRY IN TRANSLATION SERIES

THE GREAT MADNESS by Avigdor Hameiri. Translated and edited by Peter C. Appelbaum. Introduction by Dan Hecht

Of Human Carnage - Odessa 1918-1920 by Avigdor Hameiri. Translated and edited by Peter C. Appelbaum. Introduction by Dan Hecht

A Flea the Size of Paris: the Old French "Fatrasies" and "Fatras" Translated by Ted Byrne and Donato Mancini

Howls & Growls: French Poems to Bark By. Translated by Norman R. Shapiro & Illustrated by Olga Pastuchiv

RhymAmusings by Pierre Coran. Translated by Norman R. Shapiro

In Praise of Sleep: Selected Poems of Lucian Blaga. Translated by Andrei Codrescu

Through Naked Branches: Selected Poems of Tarjei Vesaas. Translated by Roger Greenwald

I Have Invented Nothing: Selected Poems by Jean-Pierre Rosnay. Translated by J. Kates

Fables of Town & Country by Pierre Coran. Translated by Norman R. Shapiro & Illustrated by Olga Pastuchiv

Earthlight (Clair de terre): Poems by André Breton. Translated by Bill Zavatsky and Zack Rogow

The Gentle Genius of Cecile Perin: Selected Poems (1906-1956) Translated by Norman R. Shapiro

Boris Vian Invents Boris Vian: A Boris Vian reader. Edited and Translated by Julia Older with a Preface by Patrick Vian

Forbidden Pleasures: New Selected Poems [1924-1949] by Luis Cernuda. Translated by Stephen Kessler

Fables In a Modern Key (Fables Dans L'Air Du Temps) by Pierre Coran. Translated by Norman R. Shapiro & Illustrated by Olga Pastuchiv

Exile Is My Trade: A Habib Tengour Reader. Translated by Pierre Joris

Present Tense of The World: Poems 2000-2009 by Amina Said. Translated by Marilyn Hacker

Endure: Poems by Bei Dao. Translated by Clayton Eshleman and Lucas Klein

Curdled Skulls: Poems of Bernard Bador. Co-translated and edited by Clayton Eshleman

Pierre Reverdy: Poems Early to Late. Translated by Mary Ann Caws and Patricia Terry

Selected Prose and Poetry of Jules Supervielle. Translated by Nancy Kline, Patrica Terry, and Kathleen Micklow

Poems of Consummation by Vicente Aleixandre. Translated by Stephen Kessler

A Life of Poems, Poems of a Life by Anna de Noailles. Translated by Norman R. Shapiro

Furor & Mystery and Other Poems by Rene Char. Translated by Mary Ann Caws and Nancy Kline

The Big Game (Le grand jeu) by Benjamin Péret. Translated by Marilyn Kallet

Essential Poems & Prose of Jules Laforgue. Translated by Patricia Terry

Preversities: A Jacques Prevert Sampler. Translated by Norman R. Shapiro

La Fontaine's Bawdy by Jean de la Fontaine. Translated by Norman R. Shapiro & Illustrated by David Schorr

Inventor of Love by Gherasim Luca. Translated by Julian and Laura Semilian

Art Poetique by Guillevic. Translated by Maureen Smith with Lucie Albertini Guillevic

To Speak, to Tell You? by Sabine Sicaud. Translated by Norman R. Shapiro

Poems of A. O. Barnabooth by Valery Larbaud. Translated by Ron Padgett and Bill Zavatsky

EyeSeas (Les Ziaux) by Raymond Queneau. Translated by Daniela Hurezanu and Stephen Kessler

Essential Poems and Writings of Joyce Mansour. Translated by Serge Gavronsky

Essential Poems and Writings of Robert Desnos: A Bilingual Anthology Translated by Mary Ann Caws, Terry Hale, Bill Zavatsky, Martin Sorrell, Jonathan Eburne, Katherine Connelly, Patricia Terry, and Paul Auster

The Sea and Other Poems (1977-1997) by Guillevic. Translated by Patricia Terry

Love, poetry, (L'Amour La Poesie, 1929) by Paul Eluard. Translated by Stuart Kendall

Capital of Pain by Paul Eluard. Translated by Mary Ann Caws, Patricia Terry, and Nancy Kline

Poems of André Breton, A Bilingual Anthology. Translated by Jean-Pierre Cauvin and Mary Ann Caws

The Water Drinkers: and Other Sketches of Paris in the Romantic Age by Henry Murger. Translated by Zack Rogow

Last Love Poems of Paul Eluard. Translated by Marilyn Kallet

Approximate Man & Other Writings by Tristan Tzara. Translated by Mary Ann Caws

Chanson Dada: Selected Poems of Tristan Tzara. Translated by Lee Harwood

Disenchanted City: La ville désenchantée by Chantel Bizzini. Translated by Marilyn Kallet and J. Bradford Anderson

Guarding the Air: Selected Poems of Gunnar Harding. Translated by Roger Greenwald

BLACK WIDOW PRESS BIOGRAPHY SERIES

Revolution of the Mind: The Life of Andre Breton
by Mark Polizzotti

Black Widow Press is an imprint of Commonwealth Books, Inc., Boston, MA. Distributed to the trade by Simon & Schuster throughout North America, Canada, and the U.K. Black Widow Press and its logo are registered trademarks of Commonwealth Books, Inc.

www.blackwidowpress.com

BLACK
WIDOW
PRESS